D1553163

HOW TO PRAY WHEN
HE DOESN'T
BELIEVE

Past. Min.

HOW TO PRAY WHEN HE DOESN'T BELIEVE

MO TIZZARD

LIFE JOURNEY®

Bringing Home the Message for Life

COOK COMMUNICATIONS MINISTRIES
Colorado Springs, Colorado • Paris, Ontario
KINGSWAY COMMUNICATIONS LTD
Eastbourne, England

Life Journey® is an imprint of
Cook Communications Ministries, Colorado Springs, CO 80918
Cook Communications, Paris, Ontario
Kingsway Communications, Eastbourne, England

First published 2001 by
KINGSWAY COMMUNICATIONS LTD
Lottbridge Drove, Eastbourne, BN23 6NT, UK
Email: books@kingsway.co.uk

HOW TO PRAY WHEN HE DOESN'T BELIEVE
© 2004 by Mo Tizzard
UK copyright © Mo Tizzard 2001

Cover Design: Two Moore Designs/Ray Moore

60743143

First North American Printing, 2004
Printed in the United States of America
1 2 3 4 5 6 7 8 9 10 Printing/Year 08 07 06 05 04

ISBN: 0781441668

Acknowledgments

My deepest thanks go to Jan Hodge, who befriended me and drew me into an awareness of the love of God, and who stood by me and prayed for Bill and myself in the struggle for his salvation.

Also, in the same measure, my thanks go to David Dixon, my pastor at that time, and his wife Jan. I so appreciate them for their love, support, and covering during that time and for their commitment to rally the church in prayer for my family. It was the backbone to the outcome recorded in this book.

Thanks, too, to all those friends in West Street Evangelical Church who prayed week in and week out, especially at the Friday night prayer meetings.

My blessings go to my two daughters, Dani and Nikki, who put up with a lot during that difficult time in our family life.

Finally, thanks and lots of love to my husband, Bill, without whom this book would not have been written!

Contents

"It's God or me!" That was the stark choice I was facing as a brand new, five-day-old baby Christian with no church background. What do you do when your husband presents you with such an incredible ultimatum? Where do you turn when an answer is expected immediately?

The answer was my first experience of total dependency on God, the God I'd met just a few nights earlier at a ladies' meeting.

The answer I needed didn't come in a booming voice or a still, small one. Nor did it come through remembering some Scripture—for I knew none. Instead, into my mind came a line from a hymn I'd sung many years ago in school: "Holy, Holy, Holy! Lord, God Almighty." So I thought, *If God is as holy and almighty as that hymn says he is, then Bill will never change God, but God might change Bill!*

So I made my choice and presented it to Bill as gently as I could. That was the beginning of a time of great pressure and discord, but a time of incredible learning from God himself in the school of the Holy Spirit.

Through the next eighteen months, under intense pressure to give up my faith, I learned what to pray, how to pray, and how to live effectively before my husband. I learned the lessons through both obedience and failure, working with the Holy Spirit until Bill was saved … and beyond.

The actions I took and the prayers I prayed were in response to what God showed me at the time. Full understanding of the Scriptures and discipleship principles came later.

The underlying theme of this book is that God wants to teach us himself, firsthand, and then confirm it through others. Thus we get "bonded" to him rather than to people, structures, or systems in our Christian lives; although the church, Christian friends, and leadership do have a vital part to play in affirmation, prayer, and support.

Although this book is primarily aimed at women praying for their unsaved husbands, it could also be useful for anyone praying for any unsaved friend or relative.

Our story is unusual and unique, and most husbands don't have such an extreme reaction to their wife's salvation. But I have found that our story encourages people to believe that God can save even the most resistant person.

CHAPTER I

New Birth—New Problems

After the "It's God or me" ultimatum and my decision to choose God in the hope that he might change my husband, to my dismay Bill began packing a bag. Our two little girls, who were then almost six and three-and-a-half years old, asked their daddy, "Where are you going?" He curtly replied, "Ask your mother!" and walked out.

I was confused. All I'd done was explain that I had become a Christian and therefore wanted to go to church on Sunday, and all this mayhem had followed. I calmed the children, got them ready for bed, and wondered what would happen next.

What happened was that my father-in-law arrived, with my husband's uncle. My parents and my in-laws had been best friends for fifteen years. I had known and loved my father-in-law since I was ten years old, and I knew he loved me as the daughter he'd never had. But here he was, angrily demanding to know what was going on and why Bill was so upset. Bill had turned up on their doorstep saying, "I don't know what's happened to Mo. She's talking about God and religion and stuff. I think she's gone out of her mind!"

I began to explain to them that I had been going to some monthly ladies' meetings for a while and that the previous Monday evening I had realized that God was real. It was when the speaker said, "Let's pray now, because I believe there is somebody here who wants to get through to God" that I said quietly in my heart, "It's me! It's me!" I began to shake all over, there was a rushing noise in my ears, my heart starting thumping, tears streamed down my face, and I sat there, while the others were still praying, watching my knees shake. *I must be ill,* I thought. *I've got the flu.* But when I eventually told my friend about it the next day, she surprised me by saying that I'd been born again—I'd become a Christian.

> Jesus declared, "I tell you the truth, no one can see the kingdom of God unless he is born again." (John 3:3)

The Gospel had never been explained to me. I thought being a Christian was connected with going to church and being a good person. The friend who came round that morning had been praying for me for months, but sensing my embarrassment at things religious, had wisely said nothing. The only reason I went to those ladies' meetings was because I valued her friendship and I didn't like to say no.

So when the speaker said, "I think there is someone here trying to get through to God," I had no idea I needed to be "born again." All I knew was that I wanted to know God!

The experience I had as the Holy Spirit came upon me was undeniable. God knew I would need that to hang on to during the testing time I was about to go through. But since then, and through talking to many others, I realize that not everyone has such an experience at the time of her new birth.

But whether you have such an experience or not, the bottom line is "If you confess with your mouth, 'Jesus is Lord,' and believe in your heart that God raised him from the dead, you will be saved" (Rom. 10:9).

The most important thing is not whether you have an experience, but to know that you are God's child and he is your heavenly Father and that you are now a part of his family.

CHAPTER 2

More Problems

"What absolute rubbish!" my father-in-law said as I explained all this. Uncle Frank just sat there quietly shaking his head in disbelief. My father-in-law then began to tell me how all this religious stuff was a scam, and how the preachers are all in it to get the money. He had been a sergeant in the army, and as he angrily ranted and raved he jabbed his cigar butt inches away from my face to illustrate his points. But I was totally unmoved and at peace. It was as if I were encased in a bubble of calm! I remained calm throughout the two hours they were there, despite the third degree. Then they gave up and went back home to report to Bill and his mom that I was a hopeless case. As soon as they left, the bubble burst and I cried my eyes out.

The next morning I went to church and cried all through that, too. I walked out of church and there, waiting in their car, were my mom and dad. Our parents had been phoning each other trying to sort out my sudden interest in God and my desire to go to church. My father-in-law had failed to deter me with his tactics, so now it was my parents' turn to try.

As we sat at the table, after a hastily prepared lunch, my father began by telling me that they'd called in to see my doctor on the way to the church. Like any good dad, he wanted to find out who and what I'd gotten myself involved with. Was it some peculiar sect? The doctor was able to reassure them that the church people were very nice and not a bunch of weirdos, but in his opinion they "went a bit too far." He assured them that it was probably just a passing phase, and I would soon snap out of it.

So Dad set about trying to persuade me to "snap out of it," to consider my husband, my children, and my marriage. He was so warm and loving and persuasive. But I suddenly realized that although the words were soft and sweet, it was the same thing that my father-in-law had said, only in disguise. They wanted me to deny the God I had just found, forget him and church, and go back to being the normal daughter, wife, and mother I had always been.

This gentle, loving approach was so much harder to cope with than the "in your face" angry words of my father-in-law. So I put my hand on his arm and said, "Please, Dad, if you love me you'll stop right now." With that he got up, picked up the phone, called Bill and said, "Bill, I think you should come home."

After a brief conversation Dad handed the phone to me. Bill was very firm: "I will come home if you don't talk about God anymore. I don't want you going to church or any more meetings, and I don't want you to have anything more to do with that woman who took you there. And by the way, if her husband sets a foot down our driveway I'll punch him on the nose!"

"Okay," I said. "I'll do everything you say. But you realize I will have to see Jan when taking the kids to school. I can't help that. And is it okay if I have a Bible?" He grudgingly agreed, and so, after just one night away, Bill came home.

> Then Jesus entered a house, and again a crowd gathered, so that he and his disciples were not even able to eat. When his family heard about this, they went to take charge of him, for they said, "He is out of his mind." (Mark 3:20–21)

Then Jesus' mother and brothers arrived. Standing outside, they sent someone in to call him. A crowd was sitting around him, and they told him, "Your mother and brothers are outside looking for you."

"Who are my mother and my brothers?" he asked.

Then he looked at those seated in a circle around him and said, "Here are my mother and my brothers! Whoever does God's will is my brother and sister and mother." (Mark 3:31–35)

Doing God's will and yet keeping relationship with your family can sometimes clash. Jesus' relatives had trouble, at the beginning of his ministry, understanding him and what he was saying and doing. They thought he was out of his mind and went to "take charge of him."

It's hard for unsaved relatives to understand, and some of them may want to take charge of us "for our own good." It's those closest to us who want to spare us the hurt and embarrassment of doing something that's going to cause a problem.

And it's those who are closest to us who have the most influence on us. Remember, it was Delilah, the woman Samson loved, who eventually wore him down and persuaded him to tell her the secret of his strength, thus enabling the Philistines to capture him and render him ineffective. It was a loved one who was used to weaken and disable the man God had chosen for his purposes (see Judg. 16:4–22).

We need to pray for the courage to be obedient and to do the difficult things that loved ones sometimes don't understand.

CHAPTER 3

Bonded to Him— by Restrictions

I was very pleased to have Bill come home after only one night apart; but although he was there, he wasn't happy. So I had to be very wise about how I behaved as a Christian when he was around. He worked very long hours in the family business, so I would take time out in the day to read my Bible and pray—children permitting, of course. But, as a busy mom, I soon learned that prayer was just talking to God … anywhere at any time.

Bill had said "no meetings and no church," but I was able to see my friend Jan on the way to school with the children every weekday. Jan was the one who had prayed for me and taken me to the ladies' meetings where I had eventually been saved. We would talk all the way to and from school—I would share what was happening with Bill and myself and she would disciple me "on the move."

Jan arranged for the Sunday messages, morning and evening, to be recorded for me and would give me the tape every Monday morning. I usually managed to hear some of it when the children were playing together after school in the afternoons. So I had discipleship and I had teaching. But I didn't have much in the way of fellowship or companionship with other Christians.

As the weeks and months went on and Bill's attitude didn't change, sometimes I thought I was a bit ill treated. But as I look back I realize it was a privilege, because my fellowship and companionship had to come from the Lord himself. It was him and me. He was the only one I could talk to during the day; the only one I could turn to for comfort or counsel, apart from the brief chats with Jan. When things were going badly, I would sometimes just put my hand up in the air as if I were a little girl taking hold of her daddy's hand. I had to go through some very difficult things during that time of restriction, but there were some very precious moments, too. And there was the sweetness of those "stolen moments" when Bill was at home and I would sneak off for a minute or two, just to talk to Jesus.

> Arise, come, my darling; my beautiful one, come with me. (Song. 2:13)

I have wondered many times why my husband reacted the way he did. I found out there were several other women in the church whose husbands weren't Christians, but they didn't stop their wives from going to church or meetings. Did Bill feel as if I had someone else? Was one of the reasons he reacted so badly based on his jealousy—someone had stolen his girl?

It says in Scripture that the Lord is jealous over his people and that he looks for our love and devotion just as the bridegroom does with his bride. But there are always demands for our attention, and sometimes our timetables get crazy, and the Lord has precious little of our time.

Many years ago I heard someone say, "We need to distinguish between what is urgent and what is important." As I thought about this I realized that often the things that are urgent will shout loudly and demand we pay attention to them, while those things that are really important are often forgotten, mainly because we are too tired and exhausted, having spent all our energies on the urgent things.

We need to spend time with the Lord, talking to him in our quiet times, but also on the move as we do some of the more mundane jobs like housework, gardening, doing the dishes, or on the way to and from work. Because the only way to get to know someone is by talking to them, and we can talk to him anytime, anywhere.

And I will ask the Father, and he will give you another Counselor to be with you forever—the Spirit of truth. (John 14:16–17)

CHAPTER 4

Bonded to Him— Through His Word

Bill had agreed to come home on the condition that I didn't go to church or to the ladies' meetings anymore. But he had agreed that I could have a Bible. "I don't see what good that will do you," he had said.

In the cupboard was an old, black King James Version of the Bible that I had been given many years ago at school, but this had always been a very formidable book as far as I was concerned. Then I remembered we had another one; it was a modern translation of the New Testament called the *New English Bible*. I was amazed as I remembered how we came to have it.

Bill and I were married in our local parish church seven years previously. We did not attend the church, but the Reverend Stuart Carne-Ross was willing to perform the ceremony. After the vows, he invited us up to the high altar for the blessing, and then he gave us a copy of the *New English Bible* to start our married life with. I can't thank God enough for him, not only for the Bible, but for the prayers that he must have prayed over it before he handed it to us. In our wedding album are photos of us walking down the aisle as husband and wife, with Bill carrying a Bible under one arm and me on the other. What a prophetic statement!

So it was to this New Testament that I turned in order to understand who God the Father is and who Jesus and the Holy Spirit are. I began to read it from front to back because I knew absolutely nothing. With a three-year-old at home during the day, and Bill at home at night, I had to snatch my moments ... but it was worth it.

As I read through my New Testament, chapter by chapter and book by book, my eyes were opened and I began to understand who Jesus is and why he had died. One day, a few months later, I saw how bad my attitudes and my self-centeredness were. I saw that, although Jesus had done nothing wrong, he was willing to take incredible punishment and die so that I could be forgiven. I sinned and he got punished.

I cried and cried in remorse as the revelation hit me. I had become increasingly aware of my shortcomings as a person, especially as a wife and mother, before my born-again experience, but now I knew them even more deeply. I had never had the Gospel preached to me or been told that I was a sinner, and if I had I would have probably denied it. But when I received that revelation of my sinfulness through his Word, I couldn't deny it.

As the tears subsided there came the sweetness of the Lord's forgiveness and the realization that he loved me despite all my shortcomings: that he'd accepted me as his child, all those months ago, fully knowing all the rubbish that was in me.

I knew then that his love was unconditional. Not because I deserved it or had earned it ... but because Jesus took the punishment for all my sins—the ones I knew about, the ones I wasn't aware of, and those I will be guilty of in the future. They have all been put down to his account ... he'd paid in advance!

> Dear children ... your sins have been forgiven on account of his name. (1 John 2:12)

Another way to describe God's forgiveness is *mercy*, and a good description of his unconditional love is *grace*. Mercy is not getting what we deserve. Grace is getting what we don't deserve!

Both in Hebrew and in Greek the word *grace* means "favor" or "gift." But the Old Testament Hebrew word for grace—*chen*—gives us an even better understanding, because it is from the root word *chanan*, which means for a superior to bend or stoop in kindness toward an inferior.

"For God so loved the world that he gave his one and only Son" (John 3:16). He sent him before we even realized we needed a Savior and before we had even agreed to repent of our sin.

The almighty Creator of the universe stooped down to our level and became like us—a weak human being—in order to show us his immeasurable kindness. In doing so he gave us the opportunity to receive his mercy, his forgiveness, and his grace—his unconditional love.

He wants us to experience his mercy and grace deep in our foundations so that the building of our Christian lives will stay firm and immovable. His love is unconditional, not based on works—what we do or don't do—but on loving acceptance. He wants us to know that we can freely come to him as a child to a loving father.

CHAPTER 5

Bonding and Backing

Before I go any further into this book, I need to tell you of the enormous debt I owe to the brothers and sisters of my church who backed and supported me in prayer. I had met some of the ladies during the time I went to the monthly evening meetings, but to others in the church I was a complete stranger. They had heard about me and about Bill's reaction when I had been saved, but many of them, especially the men, didn't even know what I looked like.

The pastor and his wife, David and Jan Dixon, lived just up the road from us, and their youngest daughter went to the same school as our two girls. But mainly my friend Jan kept the church updated with my situation and rallied extra prayer when things got difficult.

The other contact was through the Sunday school teachers. Part of Jan's strategy to get me saved was to offer to take my two daughters to Sunday school every week, and we had agreed to that quite awhile before. When I became a Christian, because Bill didn't want Jan coming to our house and I couldn't drive, he agreed to drive them to Sunday school every week himself. This always seemed ludicrous to me—he was vehemently opposed to my going to church, yet he would drive us all to the house where the Sunday school was being held. He didn't go in, so taking them in every week gave me a brief but sometimes vital opportunity to ask for prayer when things were especially difficult.

Being on the front line, so to speak, it was an enormous relief to know I wasn't on my own and that there was an army behind me.

> The Amalekites came and attacked the Israelites at Rephidim. Moses said to Joshua, "Choose some of our men and go out to fight the Amalekites. Tomorrow I will stand on top of the hill with the staff of God in my hands."
>
> So Joshua fought the Amalekites as Moses had ordered, and Moses, Aaron and Hur went to the top of the hill. As long as Moses held up his hands, the Israelites were winning, but whenever he lowered his hands, the Amalekites were winning. When Moses' hands grew tired, they took a stone and put it under him and he sat on it. Aaron and Hur held his hands up—one on one side, one on the other—so that his hands remained steady till sunset. So Joshua overcame the Amalekite army with the sword. (Exod. 17:8–13)

When praying for our unsaved husbands we may feel very much like Joshua, in the thick of it, right there in the heat of the battle. But what the Lord wants us to know is that he is our Joshua. In fact Joshua is the Old Testament name for Jesus. Joshua/Jesus in Hebrew is *Yeshua*—"Jehovah saves."

Our part is to be like Moses on the hill with the staff of God in our hands lifted up for victory. But, just like Moses, our hands get tired, and the staff in our hands, which was used to demonstrate God's authority and power, gets lower and lower. It's at this point in the story that Aaron and Hur encouraged Moses to sit on a stone while they held his hands up, one on each side.

Like Moses, what we need is an Aaron and a Hur to come alongside us, to help lift up our hands as we get weary—while we sit on the stone. The Hebrew word for "stone" is *eben*, from the root word *banah*, which means "to build." We need to be firmly seated on our foundation stone, which is Jesus. We need to be dependent, resting, abiding, and putting all our weight on him. We need to be both bonded to him and supported by our Christian brothers and sisters.

If you are alone and feeling the weight of responsibility, if you are crying out, "Lord help me, my hands are getting tired and my legs are weak from standing," make sure your weight is on him. Cry out for the Lord to stir up a new awareness in your brothers and sisters that you need their support in prayer.

But whatever you do, don't get resentful or bitter—that is just counter-productive. Pray that they will see how they can be like Aaron and Hur to you, so that while you are learning from him the part you are to play in this battle, they will be there alongside you till the victory is won.

CHAPTER 6

More of You and Less of Me

There were a few rare but important times when Bill agreed to my going to something "churchy." As I look back now I can see the hand of God in making Bill amenable just at the right times.

Four months after I became a Christian I went to hear a New Zealand lady named Joy Dawson speak at a daytime meeting. The subject she spoke on was the release of the Spirit through brokenness, and boy, was it a tough message! I still remember a lot of it today, but the point that hit me hardest there and then was this: "If they don't know you are a Christian in your own home, how will anyone else know?"

At the end of her message we were invited to stay seated and talk to the Lord regarding our lives in relationship to what had been said. As I closed my eyes that sentence rang out in my thoughts. So I said, "Lord, if they are to know that I am a Christian in my home and in my family, then there's got to be more of you and less of me."

No sooner were the words spoken than I felt that sensation of the presence of the Lord touching my life again. But this time there was no shaking or bewilderment.

A couple of days later, on the Sunday afternoon, I went for a stroll with my two daughters, leaving Bill to have a bit of peace and quiet. My stroll just happened to pass the house of my friend Jan. On the spur of the moment I decided to knock. She was really happy to see me, and she invited me in to meet her husband. When our girls disappeared off to play together, she asked me if I'd enjoyed the meeting. "Oh, yes!" I replied. "And this time I wasn't worried when I felt God's presence come upon me." Both Jan and Bob sat up. "It sounds like you were filled with the Holy Spirit. Have you found yourself speaking any strange words since then?"

I said I hadn't, so they explained that one of the gifts the Holy Spirit gives us is a new language, and would I like them to pray for me to receive that gift? I readily agreed, and after they'd been praying for a few minutes I got the courage to speak out some strange sounds that I could hear in my mind.

The girls came in from the garden and it was time to leave, but as I walked down the hill toward home, more words from that new language were rising up into my mouth. It was as if a fountain of words were spurting up from inside. I desperately wanted to let these words out of my mouth, so I knew I'd better not go straight home. I had to risk being out longer than I had planned, so I took the girls to a nearby playground, put them on the swings, stepped away, and let this new language pour out of my mouth into the empty field.

The next day, being Monday morning, Jan gave me the tape, as usual, of the two Sunday church services. On it was the pastor, David Dixon, teaching on the subject of being filled with the Holy Spirit and speaking in a new language!

> All of them were filled with the Holy Spirit and began to speak in other tongues as the Spirit enabled them. (Acts 2:4)

> Then Peter stood up with the Eleven, raised his voice and addressed the crowd. … (Acts 2:14)

As ordinary human beings we can have the best of intentions and determinations, but when the pressure is really on we are just as likely to forget those good intentions and take the easy way out.

Peter "blew it" big time when he denied knowing the Lord three times after Jesus had been arrested. Previously he had made a bold statement about being willing to go to prison and even death for Jesus' sake (see Luke 22:33), but when the pressure came and reality hit, he ran. But then a few weeks later, when he was filled with the Holy Spirit on the day of Pentecost, he stood up in front of thousands of people and told them about Jesus and their need to accept him as their Savior.

"Give me the thousands," I hear some of you saying. Sometimes it's easier to witness to complete strangers than to those we know and love. The hardest thing is trying to live out the Gospel before our own family. They are so up-close and personal, and it's impossible to be a model Christian all the time. The only thing we can do is to say to Jesus, "There's got to be more of you and less of me, Lord."

Paul told us to "… be filled with the Spirit" (Eph. 5:18). The word *be* is written in the continuous tense, which means we should read it as "be being filled with the Spirit" or "continue being filled with the Spirit." This means we need to be filled with the Holy Spirit not just once, on that initial occasion, but over and over again.

Take any and every opportunity to "be being" filled. When you feel dry and empty, ask Jesus for more of the Holy Spirit's infilling. We can't do the job—be witnesses, live the life, pray effectively—without his presence working in and through us every day.

Ask the Lord for the gift of tongues—that is, to speak in another language. It's invaluable: "He who speaks in a tongue edifies himself …" (1 Cor. 14:4). The English word *edify* means "to build up" and comes from the Greek word *oikodomeo*, which means "to be a house builder, to construct or confirm." There is no point in having good foundations if we leave it there. We need to build up our house. One good way is to read the Bible, the Word of God, and another is to talk to him in prayer. But we don't always know what to pray, how to express what we are feeling, or how to say what we think or explain what we want. The gift of speaking in tongues enables us to talk unencumbered, without worrying about phraseology. It allows our inmost being to express itself through the new language, knowing that God understands exactly what is being said.

The gift of tongues is the only gift of the Holy Spirit that we can offer back to God in worship. All the other gifts we read about in 1 Corinthians 12 are for the benefit of man only; the gift of tongues not only edifies and builds us up, it is also a language of worship to the Lord.

God Redeems Our Mistakes

How can Bill get saved if he never goes to a meeting? This was the thought that was going round and round in my head. I had been saved in a meeting, so somehow I needed to get him to a meeting, too, so he could be saved. The problem was that I couldn't go with him because I would have to stay with the children. So I would have to arrange for one of the people from church to pick him up and take him. But would he go?

"Well," I reasoned to myself, "the Bible says—somewhere—if you ask anything in faith you can have it. So I shall have faith for the faith that he will go." That was the answer: I'll have faith for faith. He will go, and then he'll be saved in a meeting, just as I was.

Can you hear the "clang" resounding in heaven as I convinced myself that this was a master plan?

Well, I'm afraid I didn't. Nor did I hear it as I told Jan of my master plan. And I quickly brushed away the doubtful query from dear Val, who was the wife of the couple I'd arranged to give Bill a lift to the meeting. After all, if you have faith—and I had "faith for faith"—it's not going to seem reasonable to the human mind, is it?

I was in for a big shock and a very valuable lesson! Val stood on the doorstep, while Nigel sat in the car (wise man!). She looked up at Bill and said, "Are you ready?"

"Ready for what?" Bill replied.

"To go to the meeting," she said.

"What meeting? I'm not going to any meeting. What made you think I was going to a meeting?" he answered.

"Oh dear!" said Val. "Mo said you were going to … um. Oh dear, I'd better be going." And with that she turned and walked back up the garden path.

"What on earth was all that about?" Bill angrily demanded, as he turned and faced me. "That poor little woman, she looked so flustered. What have you been saying to her? What's going on?"

So I, very red faced, tried to explain that I thought he would like to go to a meeting and that Val and Nigel had kindly agreed to give him a lift.

"You've gone mad!" he said. "Absolutely crazy."

And I'm afraid that was the conclusion he came to. The next day he told me he'd been talking to my dad, and they had decided that I needed a psychiatrist … and my dad had volunteered to pay the bill!

"Help, Lord!" What was I to do now? I knew I wasn't mad—just stupid!

Then out of my mouth came these words: "I'll see your psychiatrist if you'll see my pastor."

When in trouble, send for reinforcements—the bigger the better!

Bill had no desire at all to see my pastor, but my dad, being a reasonable man, thought it only fair to humor me. So, the following Sunday afternoon, with most of the church at home praying, David Dixon and his wife, Jan, came to my house and met with Bill and my mom and dad.

David was brilliant. I can't remember exactly what he said, but he managed to convince them all that I wasn't mad—which was the main thing—and that I didn't need to see a psychiatrist. He told them that it wasn't a club that I'd joined, and if they gave it a little time they would see that.

Mom and Dad were quite charmed by his quiet and gentle way, but Bill was having none of it. "Don't call me 'my dear Bill,'" he said. "And you," he said, turning to Jan, who was smiling sweetly at him, "you can wipe that grin off your face as soon as you like!"

When Mom, Dad, David, and Jan had left, I burst into tears and told Bill how sorry I was for being so stupid. Relieved that I wasn't mad after all, and seeing my obvious remorse, he cuddled me and acted quite gently toward me … for a few days.

> But each one is tempted when, by his own evil desire, he is dragged away and enticed. (James 1:14)

When we want something very badly, we are on dangerous ground. Our strong desire can open us up to being enticed into doing something stupid, and it can blind us to the truth and lead us away from the purposes of God. In my case, I was desperate for Bill to go to a meeting, because I figured this was how people got saved.

As human beings we are such copycats. We see something successful and think that's the way to do it to achieve similar success. My desire for Bill to go to the meeting was so strong that I was able to reason away any thoughts to the contrary. I was able to ignore the obvious doubts and questions of my Christian friends. And when I realized how stupid I'd been, what a bad witness I had been to Bill and my family, I died a thousand times inside.

But I've learned since then that young Christians, in learning to walk, fall over. And not just young Christians. The Enemy is always ready to put a foot out to trip us up and cause us to fall over when we are blinded by our own desires.

So, if you think you are standing firm, be careful that you don't fall! (1 Cor. 10:12)

But when we do fall over, as soon as we realize our foolish mistake, admit it, and say we're sorry, the Lord is there to pick us up, give us a cuddle, and encourage us to walk again. In fact, just like any earthly father or mother with a young toddler, he knows we are going to fall because that's how all children learn to walk. A toddler takes a few steps and then falls. He then takes another few steps and falls again. The parents don't smack their child for falling. They positively encourage him to get up and try again, knowing that he will again fall. But eventually the child is walking more than falling.

Don't forget, Jesus encourages us to be like little children, and little children fall and need to be picked up and comforted if they hurt themselves. He knew that we would fall, that we would make mistakes, that we would never be perfect. But that's why Jesus died. He died so that we could be forgiven, picked up, comforted, and encouraged to walk on.

Therefore, there is now no condemnation for those who are in Christ Jesus. (Rom. 8:1)

And we know that in all things God works for the good of those who love him, who have been called according to his purpose. (Rom. 8:28)

God doesn't just forgive us for the mistakes we make; he goes beyond that and is also able to work all things together to get some good out of our mistakes. Even if it's just that we are extremely wary of making the same mistake again and acquire a lot more wisdom for the future—a bit like putting your hand in the fire and finding out the hard way! But our loving heavenly Father is often working quietly in secret, doing things that we don't know about.

Ever since I had become a Christian, Bill had protested that he didn't need to be saved because he wasn't a sinner. But his rudeness to David and Jan played on his conscience. It made a lasting impression, and he never forgot it, because the first thing he did when he was saved was to phone David and Jan and apologize for how rude he'd been to them that day.

CHAPTER 8

Walking Wisely

After an evening of tension when negative things had been said—whether I had unwisely retaliated or just tried to avoid the issues—Bill would retreat into a heavy silence. The next day he would leave early for work and return in the evening still under a black silent cloud.

So I developed the habit of asking the Lord, "What do I say to him when he walks in the door from work?" I was absolutely amazed at what would come out of my mouth. Usually just simple things like, "Hello, love. Would you like something cold to drink?" or "How was your mom today? Is she feeling better?" I found that as I made small talk, as if nothing negative had occurred the previous evening, it completely disarmed him. He would come home expecting me to be in siege mentality or battle mode, and instead I was light and easygoing. Also, the simple questions would make him speak and break the heavy silence. So the tension would be diffused and we could carry on a reasonable relationship—until the next time.

The other thing I learned during this time was to be on my guard against retaliation, but it was a process. At first, as I realized I was about to say something I would later regret, I would endeavor to change the negative sentence mid-stream. Then I learned to swallow the words as I "tasted" them in my mouth. Then I got as far as only thinking about them. Finally, I would think, *I'm not playing that game!* and would focus my attention on something else.

> May the words of my mouth and the meditation of my heart be pleasing in your sight, O LORD, my Rock and my Redeemer. (Ps. 19:14)

Walking wisely usually means talking wisely. It's our mouths that get us into trouble all the time, isn't it? We are always putting our feet in them by saying the wrong thing. I knew someone who would say, "I only open my mouth to change feet!"

But it's "out of the overflow of the heart [that] the mouth speaks" (Matt. 12:34). The mouth is just an overflow of what we have in our hearts. No wonder the psalmist says, "May the words of my mouth and the meditation of my heart be pleasing in your sight. ..."

If we want to stop the negative words coming out of our mouths, we need to work on the attitudes in our hearts. It's no good just stuffing the words back down and then fuming inside. You know the scenario—you say nothing, but on the inside you are giving them "what for." You leave the scene quietly, but inside you are having an imaginary dialogue in which you are telling them what you think of them with magnificent eloquence.

But dwelling on the negative is giving the Enemy a landing strip. It's playing the game that he loves, and it grieves the Holy Spirit, which in turn robs us of relationship, confidence, and wisdom.

> I would rather be a doorkeeper in the house of my God than dwell in the tents of the wicked. (Ps. 84:10)

When we experience any negative event, our minds do a replay of it, over and over again. This stirs up our emotions with negative feelings and reactions. It's like dwelling with wickedness—living in the

Enemy's tent—and it makes us feel horrible. Rather, we should abide or "remain in" Jesus, as he teaches us in John 15:4.

It's impossible to leave a vacuum and try not to think about the negative, because it will always keep filling in the void. The only way to escape negativity is to think about something else and fill our minds positively.

> Finally, brothers, whatever is true, whatever is noble, whatever is right, whatever is pure, whatever is lovely, whatever is admirable—if anything is excellent or praiseworthy—think about such things. (Phil. 4:8)

One of the best ways I have found to counteract negative thinking is to think and speak blessing. If we determine to bless the person every time a negative thought comes into our mind, we will soon find those thoughts won't bother us anymore!

CHAPTER 9

Increasing Our Faith Level

I had been reading through the New Testament for months, and maybe it was that I'd reached the second part of 1 Corinthians 11, but one day I suddenly realized that I had never taken Communion. Bill and I had never gone to church except for weddings, funerals, and christenings, and so I'd never come across Communion even as an unbelieving churchgoer. And, with the ban on my going to church, I couldn't see any way I would be able to take it.

As I thought about it, there was such a longing in me to take Communion, as Jesus said, "in remembrance of" him (1 Cor. 11:24–25), that I cried out, "Lord, please make it possible for me."

A few days later Bill came home from work. "I've got to go make some purchases for the shop on Sunday. I will have to get up there fairly early, and I probably won't be back till mid afternoon, so you can go to church if you want to."

I was stunned!

As soon as Bill went out of the kitchen I rushed for the calendar, and yes, it was the Sunday morning in the month that the church celebrated Communion. I didn't really have to look. I knew in my heart that the Lord had answered my prayer before the actual date confirmed it.

That was the most precious communion I have ever taken: my very first communion, arranged personally by the Lord.

> I am God, and there is no other; I am God, and there is none like me. I make … I say … I will do … What I have said, that will I bring about; what I have planned, that will I do. (Isa. 46:9–11)

If you are in any doubt as to who is in control, read through Isaiah 40–49. Read the chapters straight off, one after another, out loud if possible. As you do this you will hear again and again, "I will," "I have," "I make," "I say," "I am," "I, even I," "I, the Lord."

We are the children of an awesome, mighty, powerful God. If you are still not convinced, read the Psalms, and listen to the response of David's heart as he meditates on the greatness of his God.

We don't always see the answers to our prayers immediately, but we know that the Lord is listening and silently planning in love for the outworking of those answers. It's not that he can't answer or doesn't want to answer. There are often greater agendas in his plan that take priority, like the building up of our faith.

The different levels of faith are like the waters in a canal. To move from one level to another we have to wait in the lock. Just like the canal barges, we have to sit between the lock gates and wait as the water is poured in. Then at the right time, when the level has risen and is equal to the water beyond, the gate is opened and the barge moves on. It takes many locks to slowly increase the level of the waters so that the journey may be completed successfully.

The increase of our faith is of greater value to our God than quick answers to prayer. For the faith that's produced will take you through and beyond that original prayer project. It will take you on other journeys to fulfill commissions and other prayer projects of his choosing.

That faith will carry you, and the Lord will use it to help lift others as they labor under their loads.

> Though now for a little while you may have had to suffer grief in all kinds of trials. These have come so that your faith—of greater worth than gold, which perishes even though refined by fire—may be proved genuine and may result in praise, glory and honor when Jesus Christ is revealed. (1 Peter 1:6–7)

CHAPTER 10

The Pray-and-Wait Tactic

We're having a baptism service at church on the evening of July second. You should consider being baptized." My friend Jan gave me the news as we walked to school one day. Me, be baptized? I'd read about baptism in the book of Acts so I had no problem agreeing with it, but how could it happen? How could I get to church for it to happen? Would Bill let me? Would Bill come and see me? After all, baptism is a witness to those around us, a witness to our faith in Jesus Christ, even if they don't appreciate the full significance of what it means. So if I was going to be baptized, I didn't want an "undercover" job, I wanted it to be known, and if possible, seen … but how?

I began to pray, asking the Lord to make Bill willing to let me be baptized, and so did Jan and the friends at church. After much prayer I summoned up the courage to ask Bill if I could be baptized on July 2. "What on earth do you want to do that for?" was the discouraging reply. I tried to explain as simply as I could and asked him to think about it. I didn't push my point; I just left it with him and continued to pray. A few days later I gently raised the subject again and asked him, without any pressure, what he thought. He grudgingly agreed that I could be baptized, but firmly stated, "But you won't get me there, so don't think you will!"

Great! This incredibly big hurdle had been overcome. "Fancy him agreeing to it, Jan," I said, as I passed on the good news. "Will he come and see you?" asked Jan. I replied, "Well, he said he won't, but who knows? God's got me this far, so I'll just keep praying and hope he'll change his mind."

The urge to "persuade" Bill was always at the back of my mind, but I knew how stubborn he could be, so I had to be very careful. And, as if he could read my mind, every now and again he would remind me that I shouldn't expect him to come. So I just kept praying. On the Saturday night before the baptism service, I casually mentioned that our little girls wanted to see Mommy baptized, and to my utter amazement, Bill said, "Okay, I'll come too."

I told Jan the next morning when I dropped the girls off at Sunday school. I can imagine how the news spread around the church that day! The infamous Bill Tizzard, who had caused such a commotion when his wife had been saved, was actually coming to church to see her baptized!

Apart from me, there were five other people being baptized that night. And before we stepped into the pool we were all encouraged to give testimony to the reason why we were being baptized. So not only did Bill hear my testimony and see me go under the water, but he heard the others' stories too!

Being baptized was the most wonderful experience. As I came up out of the water I thought my heart would burst with joy. Not only that, Bill was there, with our daughters, watching it all. He said later, after he had been saved, that he'd had a lump in his throat as big as an apple as he looked at me in my white robe giving testimony to my love for Jesus before I was immersed.

> Trust in the LORD with all your heart and lean not on your own understanding; in all your ways acknowledge him, and he will make your paths straight. (Prov. 3:5–6)

The temptation to "make something happen" is always great, especially when we want it so badly and we know someone else doesn't. Just a little word here, just a little hint there, bringing up the subject in front of someone else. Subtle manipulation, but nevertheless that's what it is—manipulation. We are all guilty of doing it one way or another. Either that or it's direct, head-to-head confrontation. But neither approach will achieve the purposes of God in our lives or theirs.

As I was writing this chapter I thought, *Why don't I use the pray-and-wait tactic more often?* Not just for an unsaved husband, but a saved one. I suppose I was more aware then of my ability to do the wrong thing and put Bill off. I was more sensitive to how things would affect him, our relationship, and the purposes of God.

The pray-and-wait tactic is something all Christians need to practice, and it's probably what Peter meant when he wrote, talking of unsaved husbands, "… if any of them do not believe the word, they may be won over without words by the behavior of their wives" (1 Peter 3:1).

Having said all that, there are times when the Holy Spirit gives us words in a powerful dynamic way. Just as he did at Jericho: after the army of Israel had walked around the walls in silence, the time came when he told them to shout!

But that's for another chapter.

Love in Action

Having prayed and waited, and been rewarded by Bill and the girls coming to see me being baptized, I found there was a further purpose involved.

Bill had seen, and briefly met, some of the Christians at the baptism service, which had enabled him to see they were just normal people, not weirdos like he'd imagined. But now he was about to find out that they were also very caring people and concerned for us as a family. That Sunday night, as they sat in church watching me be baptized, both my little girls had a very rosy glow. But I found out the next morning at the doctor's that this was because they had both contracted scarlet fever!

This meant complete quarantine for them, and obviously me, too. I was not able to take them out, and I couldn't leave them with anyone else while I went out because they were very contagious.

Bill worked with his parents in the small family business, and they all did extremely long hours to make ends meet. He left home at 7:30 AM and returned between 7:30 and 8:00 PM each night. There were no late-opening supermarkets then, and because it was a small family concern, Bill could not take time off. This gave a perfect opportunity for the people of God to show how much they cared.

For example, all my shopping was done for me by Jan, the person Bill blamed fair and square for causing all this upset. I would ring her up with a list, and she would buy the things and leave them on the doorstep, often with little extra treats included, just to bless us. The quarantine lasted for three weeks, and by the end of it Bill had to acknowledge her goodness. He tried to act indifferent, but he was definitely impacted by the expressions of love, in a practical way, from Christians.

Amazingly no one else contracted the fever, even though the girls had been sitting right in the middle of the congregation during the baptism service. Also it was amazing that neither Bill nor I realized they were running a temperature before we left the house. Because if we had, he would have had to stay at home with them. The Enemy must have tried to make sure Bill didn't get there, but God gave us both a blind spot and instead worked it together for good. In fact, the fever broke after two days, and for the rest of the three weeks they seemed perfectly normal.

> A new command I give you: Love one another. As I have loved you, so you must love one another. All men will know that you are my disciples, if you love one another. (John 13:34–35)

Any practical demonstration of Christian love speaks volumes to people and is a powerful tool for evangelism. Words on their own don't mean very much. People want to see your words in action. The wives of non-Christians are under a lot of pressure, so please not only support them in prayer, but pray also for God-given opportunities to demonstrate his love to their husbands through action.

Praying in the Dark

A s I prayed for Bill day after day, there were times when I thought, *All I am doing is repeating things over and over like a parrot. Am I achieving anything, or am I wasting my time?* So one day I asked the Lord for a Scripture verse to encourage me.

Normally the encouragements I received from the Bible were those that "jumped out at me" during my daily reading. On occasions I would open my Bible, ready to turn to the place I wanted, and have my attention drawn to a passage of Scripture before I had time to turn over. Once or twice, as a new believer, I had opened the Bible at random hoping to receive a word from the Lord. But this soon stopped when I found myself reading the words of condemnation reserved for God's enemies instead of the encouragement or direction I needed from my heavenly Father. Nowadays a few words or verses from the Bible will come into my mind, which I can then look up in a concordance and find. But on this particular day, I was given the chapter and verse to look up.

It stands as a landmark in my life, because I can only recall one other time in the whole of my Christian life when I was given chapter and verse. I hope that encourages some of you who, like me, envy those who get chapter and verse on a fairly regular basis!

When I looked up the chapter and verse I was given, it said, "We live by faith, not by sight" (2 Cor. 5:7). Sometimes our walk of faith seems a dreary trudge of repetition. We are not seeing much happen, and we are fed up and bored with praying the same old things again and again. We seem to be "in the dark." Is anything happening in response to our prayers? Well, I'll tell you this: something is happening—your faith roots are growing.

God's plan, even beyond praying for your husband, is that you become "… oaks of righteousness, a planting of the LORD for the display of his splendor" (Isa. 61:3). For an oak to grow strong and tall, it has to have a deep and massive root system, and roots grow, develop, and go deeper in darkness and drought!

The time between revelation and fulfillment is often dark and dry. It's the darkness of difficulty and dryness of inactivity. It goes in cycles, just as the seasons do. There are times of refreshing and feeding, of taking in life-giving oxygen; and there are times of barrenness and seeming inactivity. But it's in those dry, barren times that the roots are multiplying and going down into the darkness.

I clearly remember the storm of October 1987 and seeing trees that had been standing for decades, or even hundreds of years, uprooted and lying on the earth like great beached whales. They had weathered many storms over the years, but not this one. In the park near us, it looked as though a giant had strode over the land and just pushed those mighty oaks over. But the thing I noticed with the oak trees was that it wasn't the trunks that had snapped, for they were very thick and strong; it was the roots that had been severed under such great pressure.

No wonder God says that our faith is more precious than gold. It's what keeps us upright and able to withstand the strong winds of adversity.

> Who among you fears the LORD and obeys the word of his
> servant? Let him who walks in the dark, who has no light, trust
> in the name of the LORD and rely on his God. (Isa. 50:10)

The Cost

Bill and I had been married for seven years prior to my being born again. But we had known each other, through our parents' friendship, for a total of fifteen years. Bill had always been a very popular guy, as a child at school and as an adult. He and my dad were very close, and they were more like brothers than father and son-in-law. Our relationship together had been good—the usual ups and downs, but we were happy together until, as Bill always put it, "this thing came between us!"

My relationship with God provoked a kind of jealousy in Bill that made him react in a most distressing way. He adopted a policy, much like his dad's on that testing night, of trying to "shake me out of it." He began to use shock tactics of aggression in verbal abuse. I would be just sitting quietly with him, watching a program on the television, when suddenly he would say, "You're warped, you know. You are twisted. There is something wrong with you."

Wham! It was like a knife cutting into my heart!

In the confusion of this kind of attack, I would try to defend myself. But nothing I could say would convince him that it was all right to be a Christian; that it wasn't something abnormal. Instead of making things better, defending myself only made things worse.

Sometimes the constant barrage of verbal abuse, usually followed by a heavy silence, became almost intolerable.

It affected the children, too, and one day after Sunday school, my younger daughter, while sitting on her daddy's lap, said, "Daddy, do you know Jesus loves everyone—even you?" I had to turn quickly away as Bill's face revealed a look of total shock and horror. In fact it was as if she had shot him with a gun! We laugh at it now, but it was a case of Holy Spirit conviction from the mouth of a child.

If I dropped something on my toe, Bill would ask me angrily, "Why don't you swear? Normal people swear when they are hurt." Swearing in our family wasn't an everyday occurrence, only when provocation called for it, but without any conscious effort on my part I had just stopped swearing. It wasn't obvious to me, but it irritated Bill to no end.

One day while trying to insult me, although I hadn't been anywhere near a church or a church meeting, he said, "You even smell churchy!" He had no idea that he was paying me a compliment in describing what is written in Paul's second letter to the Corinthian church:

> But thanks be to God, who always leads us in triumphal procession in Christ and through us spreads everywhere the fragrance of the knowledge of him. For we are to God the aroma of Christ among those who are being saved and those who are perishing. To the one we are the smell of death; to the other, the fragrance of life. (2 Cor. 2:14–16)

The aroma of Christ, although we are not aware of it, is having its effect. That's why sometimes people take offense at us for no apparent reason and react negatively.

Paul the apostle, before his conversion, thought he was right in persecuting those who called themselves Christians: "I too was convinced that I ought to do all that was possible to oppose the name of Jesus of

Nazareth … and I tried to force them to blaspheme" (Acts 26:9, 11). He was a Pharisee and a very righteous man according to the law, but he just did not understand the ways of God. If he didn't understand, even though he knew the law, how can we expect non-Christians to understand these days? Church and God are like a foreign language to them. The unknown is often frightening and makes people feel insecure, and fear and insecurity make people act and react unreasonably. Challenged by things they don't know or understand and by different ways of doing things, people feel at a disadvantage and that affects their pride.

I am just grateful that we don't live in a society that persecutes believers. To be persecuted by someone who loves you is infinitely preferable to being persecuted by the government. But if you are going through trials because of your faith, remember, "Therefore, since we are receiving a kingdom that cannot be shaken, let us be thankful, and so worship God acceptably with reverence and awe" (Heb. 12:28).

CHAPTER 14

Counting the Cost

After weeks of Bill's relentless aggravation, his finding fault with everything I did, his constant jibes at my faith, and the hurtful comments that had worn me right down, I went into the bedroom, flung myself on the bed, and with desperate sobs said, "I can't take any more, Lord," and I meant it.

For the rest of the day Bill was quiet, and the next day he was positively nice. What a relief! In fact, over the next days and weeks he continued to be nice. It was like having back my "real" husband, the man I had known for so long and had married.

This normal state of relationship stretched on for about a month. Then one day it occurred to me that this relatively peaceful state of affairs could go on forever. But I was pretty sure that although I would still have my faith in God, Bill would jog along quite happily without any desire to know the Lord at all. And, horror of horrors, he could be knocked down by a bus tomorrow and go straight to hell, just because I wanted a peaceful life!

"Oh no, God," I cried out, "please don't let that happen. I'll put up with anything; Bill can be as horrible as he likes if it means he will get saved."

Bill walked through the door after work that night, and he was as mean and irritable as he had previously been, finding fault and getting at me for my faith. In my heart I whooped for joy! We were back on the salvation trail, but now I knew who was in control. When I'd had enough, it was as if God turned the spout off, and when I said I would put up with anything, it was as if God turned the spout back on again.

From now on the Enemy could throw anything at me, and I knew I could trust God to overrule. I knew this salvation plan was all his, and all I had to do was obey the next thing he told me to do.

> God is faithful; he will not let you be tempted beyond what you can bear. But when you are tempted, he will also provide a way out so that you can stand up under it. (1 Cor. 10:13)

Sometimes we think we have reached our limit of endurance when being put through testing times. But if that test is all part of the plan of God, he will enable us and take us past our human limitations.

> The chief priests and the teachers of the law mocked him … , "Let this Christ, this King of Israel, come down now from the cross, that we may see and believe." (Mark 15:31–32)

If Jesus had come down off the cross when he was being mocked and tested, when he was told to prove who he was, he would have saved himself, but he wouldn't have saved us!

But in the Garden of Gethsemane, Jesus had counted the cost of obedience to his Father's will before he came to the cross. I believe that wasn't the first time he had to do it. He must have counted the cost before he agreed to leave his Father's side in heaven. It was a phenomenal thing for him to lay aside his splendor and majesty to come to this earth as a man, a human being. He came, and despite the temptations, he didn't sin and so was able to present himself to his Father as the perfect sacrifice for every man's sin.

Being that sacrifice, with all that it meant in agony and pain, was not a simple thing to do; it was not a foregone conclusion even though he knew that was why he had come. He still had to count the cost for a second time there in the Garden of Gethsemane, and he still reckoned we were worth it.

The temptation to come down off the cross of God's will for our lives and to save ourselves is very strong, especially when things get really tough. But those are the times when we have to count the cost, again and again, and reckon if it's worth it.

Because Jesus stayed on the cross, enduring the shame and the pain, and because he was pierced for our sins, we have a mighty risen Savior who understands. He will help us in our weakness, take us past our own limitations, and bring us through into victory.

CHAPTER 15

Fasting

Having decided that I would put up with anything in order for Bill to be saved, a recurring thought kept coming into my mind. It was, *Maybe I should fast.* I have to admit this didn't appeal to me one bit, so for a while it remained just a thought. But then one day it occurred to me that it would be worth missing a bit of food if it was going to add a bit more vigor to my prayer life. But how could I do it without making Bill suspicious?

The answer, I decided, was to fast one day a week after our evening meal. I would miss breakfast and lunch the next day and then have my meal as usual the following evening when Bill came home. That way I would be fasting for a whole day, and he would be none the wiser.

I realized that this thought was from the Lord when, having decided to fast, my friend Jan told me the next day that she and June Shawyer, from the church, thought they might fast regularly each week for Bill's salvation. This was awesome because not only did it confirm that it was God's plan and not mine, but the amazing thing was that I hardly knew June Shawyer, and here she was willing to pray on a regular basis for my husband and fast for him too!

Because we were all busy wives and mothers, we agreed that we would all fast on the same day each week—together, but separately in our own homes.

> "Is not this the kind of fasting I have chosen: to loose the chains of injustice and untie the cords of the yoke, to set the oppressed free and break every yoke?" (Isa. 58:6)

> "You will seek me and find me when you seek me with all your heart." (Jer. 29:13)

I won't go into great detail about fasting because you can buy other books that will tell you about the reasons for fasting and its effects (such as *God's Chosen Fast* by Arthur Wallis). But I can assure you that God is in it. Luke 4:1–2 tells us that Jesus, having been filled with the Holy Spirit, was led into the desert and fasted for forty days in preparation for the start of his ministry.

There is a dual aspect to fasting: it helps loosen the person for whom you are praying from the Enemy's hold, and also it is a sign that you really mean business with God. It is not a form of arm-twisting or manipulation; it is a biblical way of saying, "This is really important, Lord, and I'm willing to go without food to show my seriousness."

There is a deeper dimension to our praying when we add fasting to it, if we are earnestly seeking after God from a willing heart. But just as praying in agreement adds more power to our praying, fasting in agreement has more power than fasting on our own.

We need to seek the Lord regarding the fast—when and how and for how long. This is important, otherwise our natural desires can take over in our effort to make something happen. This can lead to self-denial instead of a "chosen fast" and will not be effective. In fact it will just make us miserable. The "holy men" of the Middle Ages often practiced this sort of self-denial, which is called asceticism. It's what Bill and I now refer to as a "hair shirt" mentality, because these "holy men" would wear a hair shirt underneath their clothing. They thought that if they made themselves as uncomfortable as possible, they were denying the flesh and proving to God that they were more spiritual than other men!

Also, we need to be careful we don't come to God in what the apostle Paul would refer to as a "works" mentality, where we think our acceptance is based on what we do or don't do instead of who we are.

Finally, a warning for you from Isaiah 58: "Your fasting ends in quarreling and strife, and in striking each other with wicked fists. You cannot fast as you do today and expect your voice to be heard on high" (v. 4). When we go without food there is a tendency for us to become irritable. The stomach doesn't take kindly to being empty. But if we let ourselves become irritable and get into strife, we will lose the benefits of fasting, and we could actually make things worse.

CHAPTER 16

Receiving the Blueprint— Revelation

I had eagerly read the New Testament from front to back, so I was very pleased when I was able to get a hold of a complete Bible plus some Bible notes that Jan gave me, called *Daily Bread*. At some point during the day, usually when my little one was watching her TV program, I would sit down and read them.

Each day there was a passage of Scripture, which helped me concentrate on the Word and gave the Holy Spirit the opportunity to determine the theme. As I pondered on the verses for the day I often found that the Holy Spirit would highlight something he wanted to teach me or say to me. He would show me through the Scriptures what to do or how to react in a particular situation, which I would write down.

As a very young Christian I didn't really analyze how I heard from God; I was just aware of what I can only describe as recurring thoughts. They weren't anxious thoughts; they were gentle, nudging thoughts. I became aware of what the Holy Spirit was saying to me through his gentle persistence, or I would "see" what the Bible was saying to me about my particular situation. Later on I realized that it was through this gentle persistence and this "seeing" that God was able to give me step-by-step instructions or, as I call it, a blueprint for Bill's salvation.

I keep asking that the God of our Lord Jesus Christ, the glorious Father, may give you the Spirit of wisdom and revelation, so that you may know him better. I pray also that the eyes of your heart may be enlightened. (Eph. 1:17)

We need to hear from God so that we can pray and act according to his instructions. Often what most of us call "hearing the voice of God" is more like an inner "seeing" or revelation. This seeing is described in Ephesians as the "eyes of your heart" being enlightened.

Over the years I have heard many people say, "I understand it in my mind, but it needs to move down about eighteen inches so that I can understand it in my heart." But that is backward, like putting the cart before the horse. Revelation comes from the Holy Spirit into our spirits—Spirit to spirit—and then our minds are renewed to understand it. So it is heart first and then mind second, with those gentle nudging thoughts.

And be renewed in the spirit of your mind. (Eph. 4:23 KJV)

Understanding is not a matter of cramming facts, but we do need to read the Bible consistently to receive revelation, because "The entrance of Your words gives light" (Ps. 119:130 NKJV).

His Word opens or plows up our hearts, giving the Holy Spirit the opportunity to illuminate and give us revelation. So this Scripture tells us that his Word prepares our spirit to receive, not just those Scriptures that jump out at us, but also personal revelation and instruction from the Holy Spirit, the author of the Bible himself.

If it's necessary, the Holy Spirit can give us a sense of urgency if we need to act swiftly, but even in that urgency there will be a strong but gentle urging, just as a shepherd toward his sheep.

But when the thoughts that persist are not from the Holy Spirit, there is usually anxiety and a very strong compulsive pushing to do or say something immediately. There is a sense of pressure often accompanied by some confusion and fear that you must do it now or you will be in disobedience. It's so strong that you feel there is no time even to check out your guidance properly.

> But the wisdom that comes from heaven is first of all pure;
> then peace-loving, considerate, submissive, full of mercy and
> good fruit, impartial and sincere. (James 3:17)

Also with our own natural ideas and thoughts, we need to "… take captive every thought" (2 Cor. 10:5). We must give the thoughts back and give them time, because we soon forget good ideas, but the Lord's direction remains, gently nudging us in our hearts. There is a gentle, steady persistence when it is his direction.

CHAPTER 17

Receiving the Blueprint— Naturally

As a mom with young children and an unsaved husband, there wasn't a lot of time for me to sit down to pray or to hear from God. But as I moved around, doing what moms do, I would chat to the Lord, telling him how I felt about things and asking him what I should do. As I did this I would often be reminded of things I had read that morning and would have thoughts of what to do or say.

I would never have said, "I hear from God every day," because I didn't. In fact I didn't realize, till I looked back, how much of it *was* God.

After I had experienced the spout-off/spout-on situation and had counted the cost, deciding that no matter what happened or how he reacted, I wanted Bill to be saved, I found the instructions that came into my heart became more specific. Not just what to do or say, perhaps in the light of an unpleasant scene that had resulted from the previous night, but particular actions to take and ways to pray.

God was so good in that he always confirmed his instructions— which I needed after my fiasco with trying to have faith for faith! He would often confirm them through the cassette tape of the Sunday services, as he did about being filled with the Holy Spirit and speaking in a new language. Sometimes it was through a positive response from the mature Christian friends that God had given me, like Jan Hodge or Jan Dixon, as we talked outside the school. Often I could see in their faces, before they had even said a word, whether my thoughts were from God or just a bright idea. Also I observed another interesting phenomenon. Many times as I spoke to these two people—in particular about what I thought God had said—if it was only my bright idea, it was as if the words went "clang" onto the floor. But if it was what God was saying, it was as if the words took wings and flew.

Looking back now, I realize how important it was that I heard from God first and then had the confirmation through wise Christian friends. It taught me that he wants to have a firsthand relationship with us, and it helped in bonding me to him. It helped me hear his voice and taught me, through trial and error, if it was or wasn't him. I found that if I was willing to swallow my pride and be ready to admit if I had gotten it wrong, I learned so much more quickly and easily. This wasn't so hard for a new Christian, but as I got older I had to maintain it.

> And he said: "I tell you the truth, unless you change and become like little children, you will never enter the kingdom of heaven. Therefore, whoever humbles himself like this child is the greatest in the kingdom of heaven." (Matt. 18:3–4)

As the years went by I heard various sermons and read various books about the fact that I should wait on God and hear from him. With my children at school and having more time to myself, I would sit down to have my quiet time and find it was too quiet. I would get very discouraged as I strained to hear from him and heard absolutely nothing. I would become fearful that there was something wrong with me, and I would get up feeling condemned.

But the interesting thing was that as I went about my daily chores, as my mind was concentrating on something mundane like cleaning the bathroom, I would suddenly be aware that understanding was coming into my inner being—my heart or spirit, if you like. I realized that by straining to hear, I was putting myself in a place of unbelief through fear of not hearing. But when I moved about in his presence, doing what came naturally, my mind was taken up with other things, and my spirit was set free to hear.

"I will put my law in their minds and write it on their hearts." (Jer. 31:33)

CHAPTER 18

God Has a Blueprint for You

After my husband was saved, several women asked me how they should pray for their unsaved husbands. I shared with them how I had prayed, what had happened to me, and how my husband had reacted. But after a few times I began to realize that the most important thing I could tell them was, "You need to get your own blueprint from God."

Our human minds always eagerly search for the easiest and quickest route to solve our problems, to find the best methods and ways possible. But God has never been into methods and ways—his priority is relationship! Our problems should provoke us to go to him, and in seeking him for the answers our relationship with him will deepen.

In the Old Testament we see that every time the children of Israel inquired of the Lord regarding a battle they were successful. But every time they did their own thing or modeled their plan of attack on a previous victory, they were defeated.

No two battles were ever fought the same way; each battle plan was different. No two miracles performed by Jesus in the Gospels were the same, even though there may have been some similarities. No two faith ventures embarked on in modern-day times are identical. The same applies to husbands and families. Only the Lord knows the method and way to reach that man of yours. God created him, brought him to birth, and knows how to bring him to birth in the Spirit.

So take the principles offered in this book and elsewhere, but seek the Lord for the blueprint for your own particular situation. Let him guide you step by step, and in the process bring you into a deeper relationship with himself.

> Now when Joshua was near Jericho, he looked up and saw a man standing in front of him with a drawn sword in his hand. Joshua went up to him and asked, "Are you for us or for our enemies?"
>
> "Neither," he replied, "but as commander of the army of the LORD I have now come." Then Joshua fell facedown to the ground in reverence, and asked him, "What message does my Lord have for his servant?"
>
> The commander of the LORD's army replied, "Take off your sandals, for the place where you are standing is holy." And Joshua did so. (Josh. 5:13–15)

> "If you love me, you will obey what I command." (John 14:15)

Joshua's face-to-face meeting with the commander of the army of the Lord provoked a response of worship. This worship was accepted, and Joshua was told to take off his sandals, for the place where he was standing was holy. This indicates that this was not an angel he was speaking to. An angel would not accept the worship, being a ministering servant of the Lord. Joshua's encounter is what scholars would call a theophany, which means an appearance of God or a self-revelation of God.

When faced with our Jerichos the best thing we can do is worship, ask what message God has for us, his servants, and take off our sandals.

To take off a sandal was an ancient practice that symbolized the renouncing of rights: the right of possession or the right of redemption—as in the case of Ruth's nearest kinsman-redeemer (see Ruth 4:1–8).

To receive our blueprint we need to take off our sandals, renounce our rights, and give him a completely blank piece of paper to write his commands on. We need to follow and obey the commander of the army of the Lord in order to be victorious in the battle.

> This is what the LORD says—your Redeemer, the Holy One of Israel: "I am the LORD your God, who teaches you what is best for you, who directs you in the way you should go." (Isa. 48:17)

CHAPTER 19

The Importance of Praise

Living with almost constant criticism and negativity was having a depressing effect on me. I was constantly battling within myself to keep my head above water and not go under with it. When I was given a book called *Prison to Praise*, which advocated the practice of praising God in all circumstances, it helped me and made a lot of difference in my life at that time.

In reality I could not praise God for all the circumstances, but I could praise him in the circumstances—or despite them. As the criticism and accusations were leveled at me, under my breath or later on when I was alone, I would praise the Lord that he was there with me, that he knew the truth and understood everything. I was able to praise him for the fact that he never changed, that he was a great and marvelous God and always would be. As far as I could see then, it made no difference to Bill or to the circumstances, but it made a lot of difference to me in that it kept me from depression and despair, and it kept my focus on God.

> Rejoice in the Lord always. I will say it again: Rejoice! Let your gentleness be evident to all. The Lord is near. Do not be anxious about anything, but in everything, by prayer and petition, with thanksgiving, present your requests to God. And the

peace of God, which transcends all understanding, will guard your hearts and your minds in Christ Jesus. (Phil. 4:4–7)

Negativity has us chasing our tails round and round in circles. In fact it's more like a helter-skelter because it goes round and round and down and down. We need to break the cycle, and to do so we have to make specific decisions and choose to go in a different direction. We need to stop playing that negative game, and praise is the opposite of negativity; it builds faith, releases our souls from anxiety and depression, and guards our hearts.

Praise keeps our minds occupied with and focused on the greatness of our God—not just what he's done, but who he is. It lifts our eyes upward instead of inward or outward, and our focus is changed as we think about him.

Finally … whatever is true, whatever is noble, whatever is right, whatever is pure, whatever is lovely, whatever is admirable—if anything is excellent or praiseworthy—think about such things. (Phil. 4:8)

PRAISE CHANGES THINGS

I began to use praise in my prayer times for Bill. Instead of asking and pleading for God to do something, I would start thanking him for what he was doing. "I praise you, Lord, and I thank you that, even though I can't see it, you are working in Bill's life. I praise you that you are going to bring about your purposes in and through his life and eventually I, and everyone else, will see them. I praise you that you are the mighty God, and when you work no man can resist you and no enemy can stand against you."

I found that as I praised God for what he was doing and was going to do, I stopped focusing so much on what Bill was or wasn't doing, and it helped to build up my faith level.

> By prayer and petition, with thanksgiving, present your requests to God. (Phil. 4:6)

Praise and thanksgiving give power to our prayers. Praise removes the tendency toward self-pity and pleading, and it is a marvelous defense against the Enemy's weapons of despair and discouragement. The best form of defense is attack, and praise pushes back the Enemy, builds our faith, and guards our souls.

I recommend that you take some time to read 2 Chronicles 20:1–30. In this passage we get an amazing insight into the power and effectiveness of praise. The men of Judah were overwhelmed—the odds against them were massive. Not just one, but three enemies were coming up to fight them. So King Jehoshaphat proclaimed a fast and gathered the people together to seek the Lord for the blueprint for this battle. The king stood up before the assembly and petitioned the Lord, accompanied by declarations of his power and might and the great things he had already accomplished for his people Israel. Jehoshaphat acknowledged their lack of power and ability and concluded by saying, "We do not know what to do, but our eyes are upon you" (v. 12).

The Lord replied through a prophetic word and told them, "Do not be afraid or discouraged because of this vast army. For the battle is not yours, but God's" (v. 15). He went on to tell them they wouldn't even have to fight—just to take up their positions, stand firm, and see his deliverance. Their response was to fall down and worship God.

The next day the king appointed men who were to go out in front, at the head of the army, singing and praising the Lord for the splendor of his holiness.

As they began to sing and praise, the LORD set ambushes against the men of Ammon and Moab and Mount Seir who were invading Judah, and they were defeated. The men of Ammon and Moab rose up against the men from Mount Seir to destroy and annihilate them. After they finished slaughtering the men from Seir, they helped to destroy one another.

When the men of Judah came to the place that overlooks the desert and looked toward the vast army, they saw only dead bodies lying on the ground; no one had escaped. ... There was so much plunder that it took three days to collect it. (2 Chron. 20:22–25)

PRAISE RELEASES FAVOR

The word in Hebrew for "praise" is *yadah* and means "to use or hold out the hand; to revere or worship with extended hands." In Scripture the name has been anglicized into *Judah*: "This time I will praise the LORD. So she named him Judah" (Gen. 29:35). It is the tribe from which Jesus was descended: "For it is clear that our Lord descended from Judah" (Heb. 7:14).

It is no coincidence that Jesus came from the tribe of Judah, as did David, Solomon, and Jehoshaphat. All these were great kings with power, authority, and favor given to them by the greatest King of all—the Lord God Almighty.

The *King James Version* of Psalm 108:8 is, "Judah is My lawgiver," and the *New International Version* is, "Judah my scepter." The dictionary definition of *scepter* is "an ornamental rod" carried as a symbol of sovereignty.

The story of Esther provides an interesting example. Esther was a Jew, and she and her people were under threat of annihilation in the cities under the rule of the Persian Empire. She asked her people to pray and fast for three days then, at risk of her life, she dared to approach the king. He extended his scepter as a sign of her being acceptable in his presence, asked what her request was, and promised to give it to her—before he even knew what it was—even up to half his kingdom!

> When he saw Queen Esther standing in the court, he was pleased with her and held out to her the gold scepter that was in his hand. So Esther approached and touched the tip of the scepter. Then the king asked, "What is it, Queen Esther? What is your request? Even up to half the kingdom, it will be given you." (Esth. 5:2–3)

A scepter represents power and authority, and when extended toward someone, grants the person favor. In bringing our requests to God with thanksgiving and praise we are symbolically touching the scepter and all that it represents. As we praise our heavenly King, exalting and glorifying him, declaring his purposes in and through our circumstances, we not only give him pleasure, we receive his favor and can present our requests without fear.

> Let us then approach the throne of grace with confidence, so that we may receive mercy and find grace to help us in our time of need. (Heb. 4:16)

In this chapter we have looked at the power of praise and how it releases things into God's hands, allowing him to work and change disastrous situations. But we don't always feel like praising God. In fact, sometimes it's the last thing we feel like doing. The Enemy is cunning, and you may find yourself open to the charge of unreality because of this, but don't try and answer that charge. Do what Jesus did—answer the Enemy with the Word of God: "Great is the LORD, and most worthy of praise" (Ps. 48:1).

It doesn't matter how we feel. Our God is always most worthy of our praise!

CHAPTER 20

Man Is Not Our Enemy

There was never any doubt in my mind that I had married the right man. But Bill was behaving so horribly most of the time that the temptation was to treat him as an enemy. I knew this wasn't really the Bill I knew and loved, because now and again I would get glimpses of the man I married, even though they didn't last for long.

Through reading the Bible consistently I began to understand a bit more about the character and tactics of the real Enemy. One day it dawned on me that Bill was being used like a puppet on a string. His attitudes and the accusations he leveled at me were being directed by another. There was no doubt that Bill was allowing it to happen, but this revelation showed me quite clearly that I could separate Bill from the Enemy, that I could love Bill and hate the Enemy. In fact, I could be on Bill's side in hating what was happening to him.

This made an immense difference to my attitude and showed me what was going on when I was being verbally attacked. It helped me hold my temper with Bill and release forgiveness to him, because I realized that each time I retaliated against Bill it would result in the Enemy's delight at seeing us hurt one another.

They exchanged the truth of God for a lie. (Rom. 1:25)

I believe the strings that enabled the Enemy to manipulate Bill's attitudes and actions were the lies that Bill had chosen to believe. Bill was not interested in finding out the truth about God. He had no understanding of who God is or what he is like. We had never had anything to do with God or church in the past, and he certainly didn't want God or the church in our lives now. He was only interested in getting back to the way we used to live. His desire for me to give up all this "nonsense" was so strong that he honestly believed the best way to achieve this was to make things so uncomfortable for me that I would have to agree it wasn't worth it.

So by rejecting the truth about God—his motives and his character—Bill opened himself up to believe the lies that were fed to him by the true Enemy, and the result was this difficult and often distressing time.

At least I had God's company, but Bill had only the lies, so for him this time was really like hell—living with the Enemy!

HANDLING THE ARROWS OF INJUSTICE

Having seen that Bill was not my enemy, I still had to cope with the hurts and wounds that he was verbally inflicting. Because even though I understood who the real Enemy was—who was pulling the strings—I still had to deal with the fact that Bill was allowing himself to be used.

Sometimes the best way was just to duck when those arrows of injustice were being fired in my direction. I would say to myself, "That's absolute rubbish! It's not even worth a second thought." But on the days when I was feeling vulnerable and the arrows had hit the target, I needed to deal with the wounds as soon as possible so that they didn't fester into bitterness.

So I would cry out to the Lord, under my breath, for help not to react or retaliate at the moment of accusation. I would then release the pain to Jesus later on, by telling him all about it and how much it hurt, usually through my tears. Third, I would forgive Bill and declare that I still loved him and that his salvation was worth the pain! And finally, I would receive the healing and the comfort of the Lord.

In doing this I was keeping short accounts and keeping myself free from ongoing hurt and therefore bitterness. Also I was turning the tables on the Enemy, who hates healing and forgiveness.

"Bless those who curse you, pray for those who mistreat you."
(Luke 6:28)

Negative words can shape our lives and become like a curse on us. Words like "You will never amount to much; why can't you be like …?" or "You always make a mess of it; you can never do anything right!"

Cursing words are like arrows of injustice that pierce and penetrate. They are often fired by someone we love, and the more we love that person—the more significance that person has in our lives—the deeper the arrow goes in, wounding our inmost being.

If these arrows are not dealt with, they will lodge and produce pain and anger. For where you see anger you'll find hurt.

Often instead of dealing with the lies, we believe them and reinforce them by accepting them. And many of us are like those cowboys you see in westerns, who have been wounded by one or more arrows and are staggering around, still alive, with the arrows sticking out of their backs.

We need to pull those arrows out as soon as possible and break them over our knee. We do this by accepting that Jesus became a curse for us. He took all curses on himself as he hung on the cross and died with them: "Christ redeemed us from the curse of the law by becoming a curse for us" (Gal. 3:13).

Next we need to renounce the curses. The definition of *renounce* in the dictionary is "to give something up formally," "to refuse to abide by."

And finally, we need to forgive the one who fired the arrows. We need to forgive because unforgiveness is like leaving an unclean wound. It will go septic, fester, and if not dealt with, eventually bring death—in this case, the death of a relationship!

Forgiveness is like a retaliatory weapon against the Enemy. As we forgive, we release the one who has hurt us, and we strike a blow against the kingdom of darkness. Once we have done all this we can then go to Jesus and receive our healing, having exchanged those cursing arrows for his blessing.

In Isaiah 61:3 we read of the great exchange that God offers us: "a crown of beauty instead of ashes, the oil of gladness instead of mourning, and a garment of praise instead of a spirit of despair."

Chapter 21

Keeping Short Accounts

To keep short accounts" is a bookkeeping term, but it describes exactly how I knew I had to behave. I had to keep short accounts with God over my sins and not let them pile up. As soon as I realized there was something wrong and I didn't have God's peace, I would ask the Lord why. When I knew how I had sinned, I would then repent.

But as I said in the previous chapter, it was also very important to keep short accounts with Bill and others. I was not to let the hurts of their offenses, and my corresponding reactions, pile up and accumulate.

Forgiveness was something I had to learn very early on. Even without any formal teaching, I realized that I wasn't going to be able to pray effectively for Bill if I let my sin go unaccounted for, or if I refused to forgive others. If I went about the house reciting events and injustices in my head and holding them in my heart, I would get more and more irritable and short tempered, and I would lose my place of peace in God. I would be the loser, but so also would Bill and so would the children.

I learned so much about forgiveness from the wonderful story that Jesus told in Matthew 18:23–35, where a servant is forgiven a huge debt by his master, but then refuses to forgive his fellow servant who owes him only a little.

"Then the master called the servant in. 'You wicked servant,' he said, 'I cancelled all that debt of yours because you begged me to. Shouldn't you have had mercy on your fellow servant just as I had on you?' In anger his master turned him over to the jailers … until he should pay back all he owed.

"This is how my heavenly Father will treat each of you unless you forgive your brother from your heart." (Matt. 18:32–35)

One definition of forgiveness is to cease to feel angry or bitter toward or about someone, to give up the right of repayment or return for any injury.

How are we to forgive? "Just as … God forgave you" (Eph. 4:32). And how has God forgiven us? "As far as the east is from the west, so far has he removed our transgressions from us" (Ps. 103:12); "I … am he who … remembers your sins no more" (Isa. 43:25).

The way God forgives is to remove our sins out of his sight so that he can't see them, and then he forgets them. God has a good memory, but he has committed himself not to remember our sins.

"Then he is to take the two goats. … He is to cast lots for the two goats—one lot for the LORD and the other for the scapegoat. …" He shall then slaughter the goat for the sin offering for the people and take its blood behind the curtain …

"… he shall bring forward the live goat … and confess over it all the wickedness and rebellion of the Israelites—all their sins—and put them on the goat's head. He shall send the goat away into the desert. … The goat will carry on itself all their sins to a solitary place; and the man shall release it in the desert." (Lev. 16:7–8, 15, 20–22)

We see how the people's sin was forgiven by the sacrifice of the first goat. Then it was confessed onto the scapegoat, which was taken away. The sin was then out of sight and forgotten!

Do you see the parallel in that the sin of the world was paid for by the sacrifice of Jesus on the cross? But for it to be effective, we must confess our sin onto Jesus, who is also the scapegoat—the One who takes the sin away. Then our sin is removed and forgotten. He took our sin further than the east is from the west. He took our sin away into his death and out of sight!

In order for us to forgive others, we must speak out those sinful hurts onto Jesus, the scapegoat, and let them also be taken away by him into his death and out of sight. Then it's up to us to choose not to remember them anymore.

Human forgiveness often waits to see some change. If there is none then forgiveness is not given. But God does not forgive us because we do something right. He forgives because Jesus was willing to be both the sacrificial goat and the scapegoat—to die for our sins and to take them away. Forgiveness is not a reward. Forgiveness is a gift; it is grace; it is unearned favor.

The reason why God extends forgiveness to us, and why we should give forgiveness to others, is because it is an expression of the value of relationship. Jesus died because he wanted to have relationship with us. So if we don't value the relationship, we won't forgive.

But the price of unforgiveness is very high. If we refuse to forgive someone—anyone at all—we will be handed over to the jailers! The Greek word for jailers is *basanistes*, which means "a torturer" and "a tormentor."

There is a spiritual law that operates just like the physical laws of sowing and reaping. If we put someone in jail—lock them out of relationship through unforgiveness—we too will be put in jail to endure pain, toil, and torment.

Unforgiveness is so serious that it is compared to murder: "Anyone who does not love remains in death. Anyone who hates his brother is a murderer" (1 John 3:14–15).

Ask the Lord if there is any unforgiveness in your heart toward anyone at all. Ask him to expose it so that you can repent of it, let those concerned out of jail and get out of jail yourself—away from those tormentors. This will remove one of the major and most common blockages to seeing the purposes of God come fully into being. Forgiveness and love are the spiritual weapons that release God's power!

Choose to forgive—it's an act of the will, not a feeling! Don't wait for other people to change or apologize—get out of prison yourself.

Forgiveness is not always an easy or an instant thing, so to help you here are some steps to forgiveness. When they have been put into practice by a sincere heart, they can have a dramatic effect in releasing people who have found themselves tortured in the prison of unforgiveness.

STEPS TO FORGIVENESS

1. Forgive specifically—name names and state the sin.
2. Ask God to forgive you for the sin of unforgiveness and to take you out of prison.
3. Ask God to empty out the stored-up emotions—like emptying a reservoir. We can't command emotions to cease; it takes time. Remember that forgiveness is a process.

When Peter came to Jesus and asked, "Lord, how many times shall I forgive my brother when he sins against me?" Jesus answered, "I tell you, not seven times, but seventy-seven times" (Matt. 18:21–22). That makes 490 times! All for different incidents, do you think? Or maybe for the same incident!

4. Don't talk about the offense anymore. That would be like picking

the scab off a healing wound! If the mind does a replay of the incident, then the emotions follow the thoughts and will fill up what you've just emptied out!

5. Consciously work on how you think about the person concerned. Don't leave a vacuum by trying not to think about them, or negativity will move in. If you can't think of anything positive, think about or write down what you think God would like to do for them.

6. Ask God to bless that person. Ask for mercy not judgment. Nothing may change and God may choose to do nothing, but then it's his choice—because you have let them go!

7. Lastly, make forgiveness a way of life!

CHAPTER 22

Discerning God's Opportunities

I learned to discern God's opportunities mainly through trial and error. I can't remember all the mistakes I made in this process, but there were many. Like the times when I would tell Bill things I thought he ought to know, in such a way that, instead of enlightening him, I would alienate him. Or the times when he would ask me a question about God or Christian things in a sarcastic way and I would be stupid enough to respond in a similar vein. Or the times when he would ask me a question and really want to know, and having given him the answer, I would decide to add a few more insights or pointers that would cause him to back off again.

Also there were the many, many times when I would retaliate and get into a row with him as a result of the hurt he had inflicted on me. I would long to grab my hurtful words, stuff them back in my mouth and swallow them—but it was too late. They were out and had caused the damage!

Over time, however, I gradually began to recognize when Bill was asking a question that he really wanted to know the answer to. His eyes and his whole countenance seemed clear and open. But when he was just provoking me, being sarcastic and critical, his eyes and his face were darkened.

As I pondered this, with the aid of the wisdom of the Holy Spirit, I realized that Bill's eyes were like a doorway to his soul. When he was being sarcastic and critical, it was if an iron shutter were pulled down and locked over that doorway. But when he really wanted to hear and to know about the things of God and his kingdom, it was as if the shutter was lifted.

Through this understanding I learned if and when to approach Bill on a touchy subject, and also when it was wise to enter into a debate when replying to one of his questions, or if it was better to let it go by with just a casual comment. I also learned to recognize exactly when the shutter went down during a conversation. I could be talking to him, maybe answering a genuine question, when suddenly the shutter would go down. I found that if I continued and persisted in talking about Christian things after that, it would be a waste of time and could even deteriorate into an argument.

This "shutter" was so strong that if I tried to force an issue while it was down I would achieve absolutely nothing. Once it was down it would be locked tight; and in most cases, if I persisted, I would suffer severe bruising and pain to my own soul as I threw myself against it. But when the shutter was up, I had both communication and relationship with the husband I loved and who, in those moments, I knew still loved me.

> "Your eye is the lamp of your body. When your eyes are good, your whole body also is full of light. But when they are bad, your body also is full of darkness." (Luke 11:34)

It's been said that the eyes are the window of the soul, and I believe this is what Jesus is referring to. What I perceived as a doorway is what Jesus calls a lamp. But either analogy will do, because the principle is the same. Without the light of the Gospel on the inside of us, we are in the dark.

The apostle Paul wrote in 2 Corinthians 3:16 not about a shutter, but about a veil being over the minds of those who are under the old covenant of law: "But whenever anyone turns to the Lord, the veil is taken away."

Whatever analogy or terminology we use, the fact is that whenever people turn to the Lord, or as unbelievers ask genuine questions, they open themselves up to receive his light. So we need to discern those God-given opportunities and the prompting of the Lord in speaking about the Gospel, but we also need to be aware if the shutter is up or down regarding the timing.

My husband often says to people in difficult relationship situations, "In baseball, you don't swing at every ball that is pitched to you—you let some go by!" The point of this being that sometimes it is wiser not to respond to every comment you hear. Some comments are deliberately aimed at provoking you. If you respond to them rashly you risk being struck out!

It takes time and practice to discern God's opportunities, and self-control to avoid or let go those that are not of him: "Solid food is for the mature, who by constant use have trained themselves to distinguish good from evil" (Heb. 5:14).

CHAPTER 23

Abiding

I began to realize that my emotions were up or down according to how Bill was at any given time. If he was in a fairly reasonable mood, I had a measure of peace and stability. But if he was in a turbulent mood, then I would be liable to act and react wrongly. This may seem obvious. We are all affected by those we live with, whether it be a husband or anyone else in the family. But it became quite clear to me that if I could stay level and keep my own peace, it wouldn't matter whether Bill was emotionally up or down—I would be okay.

It wasn't something that happened overnight, but by trial and error I began to try to choose my reactions rather than just be awash with them as before. Learning to praise God in the circumstances helped a lot. I would say under my breath, "Thank you, Lord. You are still in control. You knew Bill would react like this before it happened. It hasn't changed you, Lord. Please help it not to change me." It didn't always work. There were days when I was still overtaken by negative reactions, but the more I took control of myself first, the better I became at it.

"I am the vine; you are the branches. If a man remains [KJV = abides] in me and I in him, he will bear much fruit; apart from me you can do nothing." (John 15:5)

In staying level, as I called it, I was actually abiding or remaining in Jesus. I was staying in my place in the Lord, in a state of peace, despite the fluctuations of our relationship or the way Bill expected me to behave or to react.

Peter tells us that our "enemy the devil prowls around like a roaring lion looking for someone to devour" (1 Peter 5:8). If a lion roared we would jump out of our skin! In the supernatural, our adversary likes to roar like a lion in order to make us jump out of our place of abiding with the Lord. He wants to frighten us into an emotional response that will either paralyze us, cause us to back off, or to do or say something we will later regret. In other words, he wants to make us anxious, unfruitful, and unproductive.

> "Do not weep! See, the Lion of the tribe of Judah, the Root of David, has triumphed." (Rev. 5:5)

But our Lord and Savior, Jesus Christ, the Lion of the tribe of Judah, has triumphed. Our wonderful Lion who is worthy of our praise has fought the roaring lion and won!

We need to ask him to show us how to get ahold of ourselves, to keep ourselves level, not letting our emotions jump in and respond before we have had time to think. We need him to help us to "be self-controlled and alert," ready to resist the fearful roar, "standing firm in the faith," so that we may become like him— "the righteous are as bold as a lion" (Prov. 28:1).

The Hebrew word for *abide* is *liyn,* and it means "to stop, to stay permanently, to be obstinate, to continue." That word *liyn* sounds just like "lion" to my ears. We need to be *liyn*, we need to be obstinate, about remaining in him when that lion roars, in order that we may bear much fruit.

Once more in this type of situation I found that praise came to my aid. It is a great help in keeping us in that place of abiding. It helps us to keep focused and to continue trusting in the Lord. It helps us to stay in our place of confidence and be obstinate about how great our God is in the face of emotional upheaval.

CHAPTER 24

Abiding in Truth

O ne of the easiest ways I could be moved out of that place of abiding, that place of peace in the Lord, was through accusation. This is because accusation, although usually unjust, sometimes contains a bit of truth in it. It's that little bit of truth, like the bait on the fishing line, that causes us to swallow the hook of condemnation. At first I would refute the accusation, then I would recognize that little bit of truth, swallow the hook, and lose my peace.

The only way I knew how to get back my peace was to cry out, "Holy Spirit, please speak truth to me." This is one of my favorite prayers, and I am always recommending it to others.

> "And I will ask the Father, and he will give you another Counselor to be with you forever—the Spirit of truth." (John 14:16–17)

> "But when he, the Spirit of truth, comes, he will guide you into all truth." (John 16:13)

He is the only one who knows the truth, and without truth we cannot have peace with God; we cannot abide or remain in the Vine. It's no coincidence that Jesus speaks to his disciples about the Father giving us another Counselor in John 14 and then immediately speaks about abiding in the Vine in chapter 15. We cannot abide without the Holy Spirit speaking truth to us.

Deception and condemnation are the weapons of the Enemy, which he uses through the minds and mouths of people. It's deception that stops us, in the first place, from seeing and admitting our sin and so entering into a relationship with our loving, but righteous, heavenly Father. If that doesn't work, the next thing the Enemy tries is to deceive us into not being honest with ourselves regarding ongoing sin, and so keeps us hiding, instead of abiding in God. And if that doesn't work, the Enemy will use condemnation to keep us locked up and ineffective by insinuation.

So we need to cry out for truth, for the Holy Spirit to illuminate the darkness and reveal any deception and to sort out the confusion that condemnation brings. Is it me? Is it him? Is he right? Am I wrong?

If we have committed any sin he will show us exactly what we have said or done. Then we can repent of it, apologize where appropriate, and receive his peace again.

When the Holy Spirit comes in truth, he takes no person's side, only the side of truth. He comes in a gentle way, a clear way. The confusion lifts, and you know what to do—to repent for your part if that's necessary, to refute the injustice in the accusation, and to forgive the person who was used to perpetrate it.

The difference between condemnation and conviction is that condemnation attacks your personhood (who you are, what you are like), but conviction points out what you have done.

Conviction is the Holy Spirit saying, "You have made a mistake." Condemnation says, "You are a mistake!"

Condemnation implies that we are the problem and seeks to disqualify us on the basis of our personality, who we are, what we are like: "You are stupid! Fancy doing that! You should have known better!"

If we agree with the condemnation—"Yes, I am stupid. I should have known better"—along comes shame, and it overwhelms us. So we repent, but we don't feel forgiven because we feel we don't deserve it. We want to do something to make it better, but we can't; to promise we will change, but we can't. Although forgiveness is freely offered, we don't accept it, and so, feeling ashamed, we hide from the Lord's presence.

> Let us throw off everything that hinders and the sin that so easily entangles, and let us run with perseverance the race marked out for us. (Heb. 12:1)

Condemnation wants to stop us running, to disqualify us from the race. But the Holy Spirit convicts us of our sin by presenting the facts of what we have done, knowing there is a solution—repentance and forgiveness through the blood of Jesus—and he expects us to take it.

Forgiveness is given not because we deserve it—none of us does—but because Jesus took the punishment for all of our mistakes. If we could have done enough to earn our forgiveness, then Jesus needn't have died!

When Adam and Eve sinned they were ashamed; they realized they were naked and tried to cover up themselves with fig leaves—which are very prickly, apparently! Then they hid from God, but when he found them, what did he do? He covered them with soft garments of skin. But to obtain those garments an animal had to die! In their shame they felt they had to hide from God, but he in his mercy saw to it that blood was shed to cover them after they had sinned! And it's only Jesus' blood that can cover us when we sin.

That is the only basis for forgiveness. We can never earn it, and if we want to abide in him instead of hiding from him, we need to pray, "Holy Spirit, please speak truth to me."

CHAPTER 25

"I Don't Think I Love My Husband Anymore"

I remember so clearly the day when I got to the end of myself. I had been separating Bill out from the Enemy—loving him and hating the one who was behind it all, pulling the strings. I had given Jesus all my hurts as they had happened, and had forgiven Bill, not letting bitterness develop and take root in my heart. But this day I came to the end of myself. I had taken so much, and I honestly didn't know if I loved Bill anymore.

I couldn't go on. I couldn't keep pushing through, putting up with the constant tension, living on pins and needles, trying my best to do the right thing and being devastated when I didn't or it wasn't enough. I couldn't go on without any response from Bill, no words of gentleness or love. And I couldn't go on without love for him. I wept and wept as I poured out my heart before the Lord. "I can't love him anymore, Lord. You'll have to love him through me!"

As my tears subsided a thought came to me that was really bizarre and out of context, but later I realized it was God speaking to me and not my own thinking. He was saying, "Go and weed the front garden." So, perplexed, I did exactly that.

It was still sunny when Bill came home after work that evening. I was at the front door to meet him, and as he got out of the car he looked around at the neat flower borders. "You wonderful girl!" he said. "You've weeded the front garden. I've been so busy and so tired and I was worrying about when I could ever get around to doing it." And with that, he threw his arms around me and gave me a big hug and a kiss. My heart burst open, and suddenly love for him just flowed out of me again.

> The only thing that counts is faith expressing itself through love. (Gal. 5:6)

Love energizes faith, making it active, efficient, and powerful. You will find a full description of what love is in 1 Corinthians 13, which shows us that love is not just the emotional, physical thing that romantic novels and films portray. But even so, it is hard to love someone when there is no warmth, when love is not given back in return, and when there is constant tension and edginess.

But blocking out love blocks faith too! I think of love being like a drainpipe that allows faith to flow through it, channeling it where it should go, but if it's blocked up the faith can't flow.

Another analogy I think of is that love is like a vehicle transporting faith to its destination. But the vehicle breaks down sometimes, so we must take it to the Lord, because he's the only one who can fix it!

> "But I have prayed for you, Simon, that your faith may not fail. And when you have turned back, strengthen your brothers." (Luke 22:32)

I cried as I wrote this chapter and relived that devastating experience. I cried for myself then, and I cry now for others who are desperate to keep their marriages together: those with non-Christian husbands, and those whose husbands know the Lord but whose marriages are going through a really bad patch.

Our human resources run dry and our human emotions get weary.

We fight against the natural reactions of the flesh to get even and often fail miserably. It's impossible to be a superwoman. We can and must do our best, but there are times when we feel we can't go on.

My only advice to you is to be totally honest with yourself and with God. Let him take you past your limitations, for you surely won't be able to do it on your own. He alone is the source of our strength and the source of all wisdom. We need help and counsel from others alongside us, but only he can see both sides. Only he can give us the specific instructions we need to carry on. Only he is on both sides at once, loving the husband and wife deeply and equally. Only he can help us deal with the hurts and injustices that we dish out to one another. Only he can show us how to separate the wheat from the chaff in our disagreements, helping us to hold on to that which is worth keeping and to let go of that which needs to be blown away by the wind of his Spirit.

CHAPTER 26

Submission—a Heart Issue

The word *submission* kept coming to my mind. As I thought about it and talked to the Lord about it, I began to realize that he wanted me to be totally submissive to Bill in all things. Now, I wasn't a rebellious, headstrong person, but I wasn't a doormat either. I knew my own mind and would argue the toss when I thought it necessary. But I grew more and more convinced that God was asking me to be very submissive. This was to be done willingly, in the right attitude, and not begrudgingly or with gritted teeth. It was to be for the Lord's sake.

So, from that point on, I agreed to any and every decision that Bill made. I did everything that he wanted me to. I didn't argue or push my point of view, but just said okay. I didn't make a show of it though, exaggerating it so that he would notice my submissive attitude. I just did what I had to. Some days it would be very hard, and all that was within me wanted to scream, but I had to keep giving those feelings to the Lord.

Then after about a month of this I had a strong impression that, having done everything that Bill had wanted me to do, now I was to do everything that the Lord wanted me to do, no matter what Bill said. This was scary!

The next day I had a phone call from Jan. There was a lady who had been staying overnight at Jan's house, who had prayed for her husband for seven years before he had become a Christian. That morning Jan had told her about my situation, and although she had to travel home shortly, she asked if I would like her to drop in and see me for ten minutes. In that short time she told me to be careful that I didn't obey the Enemy through Bill as a non-Christian, and she confirmed the call to submit to God. I was also given a very clear Scripture, and both Jan and Jan Dixon were in agreement too. So with all my safety factors in place I was ready for complete submission to God and all that it might mean.

> Wives, submit to your husbands as to the Lord. (Eph. 5:22)

Over the years I have heard sermons and read books about submission, and heard many opinions about it too. To some women the word *subjugation* springs to mind when thinking about submission, but if it is done "as to the Lord" it has a powerful effect.

It's not only women who are called to submit. Jesus was very impressed with the centurion in Luke 7, who sent for Jesus when his servant was very sick and about to die.

As Jesus approached the his house the centurian said, "Lord, don't trouble yourself, for I do not deserve to have you come under my roof. … But say the word, and my servant will be healed. For I myself am a man under authority" (vv. 6-8). It goes on to say that Jesus was amazed at the man's faith and his grasp of the submission principle. The centurion recognized Jesus' authority and placed himself under it. In this way he released a greater measure of faith.

Also, I believe that the famous spiritual warfare passage in Ephesians doesn't begin in chapter 6, verse 10. I think it begins in chapter 4, verse 17 and goes on through chapter 5 and concludes in chapter 6. Paul's instructions to the Ephesians on lifestyle and attitudes and right submission to one another are the keys to combating and countering our selfish nature, and they are designed to bring us into a lifestyle that will protect us and release us into more faith.

There is power and protection for us women as we submit to our husbands as to the Lord. It has to be a submission that's from the heart, with understanding, because we want to be as effective as possible. But if there are times when submission to a non-Christian husband clashes with submission to the Lord, then we must, in all humility and wisdom, put the Lord first. There must be no trace of rebellion or independence, but an obedience and dependence that, as we do what the Lord asks us to do, he will take care of the consequences.

"Sacrifice thank offerings to God, fulfill your vows to the Most High, and call upon me in the day of trouble; I will deliver you, and you will honor me." (Ps. 50:14–15)

CHAPTER 27

Relinquishment

At first there was no clash between submitting to Bill and submitting to the Lord, but the testing time was soon to come. It came when the Lord made it clear to me that I should go to the monthly ladies' meeting the next evening. Remember—it was at one of those meetings that I had been saved and started the whole thing off! So the next morning, as gently as I could, I explained to Bill that I was sure that the Lord wanted me to go.

"Well, I don't want you to," he said, expecting me to say okay.

"I'm sorry, Bill, but I am going," I replied.

"What!" he roared. "How do you expect me to become a Christian if you upset me by doing things that I don't want you to do?"

It must have been a real shock for him, apart from what I was actually saying. It had been quite a while since I had done anything he didn't want me to, and he must have become used to it. I suddenly saw why I had had to be very submissive to him.

"Bill," I said, as gently as I could, "you may not have realized it, but I have been doing everything you have wanted me to for the past month, and it hasn't made you any happier. So now I am going to do everything the Lord tells me to do because it can't make you feel any worse."

With that he had to leave for work and so did I. It was the one day of the week that I worked while my mom looked after the children.

During the day my mind kept straying to what I was about to do, and during the lunch hour I found myself completely alone in the office. I sat and prayed for the strength to carry out the Lord's will and go to the meeting that evening. As I sat there a scenario came into my mind with words that went like this: *Do you realize that as soon as you leave the house tonight, Bill will pack his bags and the children's, and he will leave you and take the children with him? If you go to that meeting tonight you will come home to an empty house!*

Oh no! I hadn't thought of that. He had packed a bag and left me when I had chosen God instead of him in the beginning, so it was perfectly feasible he'd do it again. But this time he could take the children with him—and I wouldn't be there to stop him. What was I going to do?

As the tears rolled down my face and my heart broke at the thought of what obeying God could cost me, I said, "Lord, if he leaves with the children tonight, he will probably take them to his mother's house. I know she loves them as if they were her own, and she would care for them and look after them as I would. So, Lord, I will go and I will trust you to take care of them for me."

So I went to the meeting that night, and when I got home there they were, sound asleep in their own beds, and Bill was sitting, disgruntled, in our living room, waiting for me to return.

> "My soul is overwhelmed with sorrow to the point of death. ...
>   My Father, if it is possible, may this cup be taken from me.
> Yet not as I will, but as you will." (Matt. 26:38–39)

Nothing can compare to the sacrifice that Jesus made for us. He was born into this world in order to give up his life for us. During that testing time in the Garden of Gethsemane, as he contemplated all that was before him—the beatings, the torture, the crucifixion itself—he was totally honest with his Father. He was the Son of God, but he lived in a body of flesh that felt pain, just as ours does. He knew the Scriptures thoroughly, so he knew, by reading Isaiah 53, exactly what lay ahead of him. He faced the cost of our salvation and still went ahead and said, "Not my will but yours, Father."

There are times in our lives when we are faced with impossible situations. There are times when the cost of obedience seems too high. Those are the times when we can hold on to what seems valuable, do the thing that seems most sensible, or we can be obedient. But to be obedient will sometimes involve relinquishment.

In the Garden of Gethsemane, through relinquishing his will and his rights, Jesus broke the power of the Enemy to control by fear. For when anything is relinquished, given into our Father's hand, it is no longer ours, and the Enemy can no longer use it against us in fear.

In actual fact, I didn't have to give up my husband and children. But as I sat there at my office desk and pictured that scene and realized what could happen, it was as real as if it were actually happening. The worse thing that could ever happen, the loss of my most treasured possessions, happened that day, in all but fact. But from that point on, they were in God's care, and I could now get on with the next thing that he would tell me to do.

CHAPTER 28

The Big Step

"Well, so far so good!" I was talking to Jan Dixon outside the school as we were waiting for our children. "I've done everything the Lord has asked me to do so far, but I'm dreading God telling me to go to church. That would certainly stir conflict with Bill!"

"But dear," Jan replied, "the Word of God tells us that we should go to church. Shouldn't you be asking him if it's right that you're still *not* going?"

Wham! Those words hit me like a ton of bricks. Here I was dreading the repercussions of being told to go to church, and secretly being relieved that the directive hadn't been given, when Jan pulled the rug out from under me.

I went home with the children, and when they had settled down to play I went into the bedroom and picked up my Bible and my Bible notes. There in the past three days' readings I saw, again and again, indications that "the big step" had arrived. I realized that, in my desire not to face it, I had turned a blind eye to it all.

So this was it: I was to go to church despite whatever Bill may say or do!

"I'm going to church this morning, Bill. In fact, I believe God has told me that I'm to go to church every week from now on." I spoke quietly and as gently as I could because I didn't want him to think I was "throwing down the gauntlet"—challenging his authority and position as my husband. But it had to be said because I couldn't just run out the door and go. It wasn't going to be a one-time event.

"Well, I don't want you to go. You are really asking for trouble now, you know. This is going too far!" He turned angrily and walked away, and I was left in the kitchen, thinking, *What's going to happen now?*

I knew that if I even thought about what could happen in the next minute, I'd be paralyzed with anxiety. So I told myself, *Don't think beyond the next second. Think about something else.* All the lessons I'd been learning about praise and about thinking on "whatever is lovely," and so on, from Philippians 4:8 were needed more than ever. So I managed to get through the next hour or so, while Bill walked around the house like a big, black, silent thundercloud giving me threatening looks.

I sat in church for the first time since I'd been baptized, and sobbed as quietly as I could. Why did it have to be like this? Why did he oppose everything that had to do with God and the church? What was going to happen when I returned home?

There was no joy in being there. I don't remember a word of what was said or what went on. It was just a step of pure obedience.

After the service Jan took me and the children home, and as I walked through the door Bill said angrily, "About time! We're due at my parents' for lunch shortly, or have you forgotten?" We jumped in our car and we were off. He was silent all the way, but at least he was there. He hadn't packed a bag and gone without us. *Thank you, Lord!* I prayed.

And to top it all, because we were at his parents' for the rest of the day, as he talked to them he found himself including me. So having broken the silence while we were with them, he carried on as normal after we left, as if nothing had happened. God's timing for me to take that "big step" and go to church couldn't have been better!

> "Be strong and courageous, because you will lead these people to inherit the land. … Do not be terrified; do not be discouraged, for the LORD your God will be with you wherever you go." (Josh. 1:6, 9)

My fear of taking that "big step" of obedience and actually going to church prevented me from hearing clearly from God. So, having failed to get through to me, he bypassed my fearful mind and heart and used my friend. Because the Lord knew that underneath the fear my heart wanted to obey him and I was willing to count the cost.

When God spoke to Joshua telling him to "fear not," he wasn't saying, "You won't be able to take this land if you are fearful." He was saying, "Don't look at the fear but look at me—for I am with you."

Naturally there is fear in our hearts sometimes, especially when we think of the possible consequences of our actions. But those are the times when we need to be obedient—even while our knees are still shaking—to do what we have to do despite the fear, and leave the consequences with him.

The Enemy will always try to discourage us in any way he can. Remember when the children of Israel had left Egypt and Joshua went in with eleven others to spy out the Promised Land? Only he and Caleb had believed that it was possible to take the land. The other ten spies had said, "But the people who live there are powerful … We seemed like grasshoppers in our own eyes, and we looked the same to them" (Num. 13:28, 33).

They assumed that because to themselves they seemed like grasshoppers in comparison to the giants, they must look like grasshoppers to them too. So they told the people not to go into that hostile place. But Joshua and Caleb tried to persuade the people to go ahead and fight, despite the giants, because they trusted that if God had told them to go in and possess the land it was possible to do so. The people listened to the other ten spies, and because of this they ended up wandering around in the wilderness and eventually dying there. It wasn't until they were all dead that their children, plus Joshua and Caleb, eventually took the land—forty years later!

It's the power of our own imagination that defeats us every time, before we even start. God knew how weak and small they were in comparison, before he told them to go in and possess the land. He knew that in their weakness they would have to depend on him, which is the safest thing to do. And it is the same for us now.

> God chose the foolish things of the world to shame the wise;
> God chose the weak things of the world to shame the strong. He
> chose the lowly things of this world and the despised things—
> and the things that are not—to nullify the things that are, so that
> no one may boast before him. (1 Cor. 1:27–29)

When the Lord says to go, or do, or say something, he already has a plan worked out to take care of the consequences—a plan that we don't always see or hear or understand beforehand. I could never have imagined that by the end of that day things would have been so relatively normal. We have to stop our imaginations from taking over, focus on him, and despite our shaking knees, do it. And do it again, if necessary. For me that was only the first Sunday of many!

CHAPTER 29

Information and Revelation

"Guess what!" Jan said. "Joy Dawson is over in this country again, and she's speaking at a meeting about how to pray for unsaved loved ones." Joy Dawson was the lady I had heard who challenged me with, "If they don't know you're a Christian in your own home, how will anyone else in the world know?" This resulted in my being filled with the Holy Spirit after saying, "Then there has got to be more of you and less of me, Lord!" A great excitement came over me, and I knew that I should go to this meeting.

When the day came Joy began by telling us that this was her last meeting in England, and the next day she was flying home to her family. She went on to say that she had been distracted with thoughts of home, and the Lord had convicted her that she was putting herself before his purposes. The subject of the message that she had spoken previously, when I was filled with the Holy Spirit, was the release of the Spirit through brokenness, and she obviously believed it and lived it out. She believed that God's power is effective as we are open and broken before both him and his people.

Next she told us that behind the meeting hall, in another room, was a group of ladies who were going to be interceding throughout the whole time that she was bringing God's Word to us. I don't think I have ever been in a meeting as powerful as that. The combination of broken-ness and intercession released a spirit of revelation that I can never thank the Lord enough for.

As Joy went through the points on how to pray for an unsaved loved one, I can only describe it as a three-cornered tennis match. She would speak each point with power—whack!—to me (and everyone else). Then I would say, "Yes, Lord, do that!" Then he would give the anointing to her to deliver the next point.

I am a compulsive note taker, so as she spoke I was writing it all down as fast as my pen would go—I didn't want to lose one bit of this message. Some of it was about ways to pray, and some was about ways of relinquishment or overcoming obstacles to answered prayer. When the meeting was over and we were driving home, I said to the ladies I was with, "There is no way that Bill is not going to be saved!"

> Then the LORD replied: "Write down the revelation and make it plain on tablets so that a herald may run with it." (Hab. 2:2)

The message I heard that day increased my faith by leaps and bounds. I found out, many years later, that Joy had battled and prayed for her son and that, since then, he has been and is being mightily used of God with an international ministry around the world. We have all heard messages that give purely head knowledge, but when the message is being delivered by someone who has lived it out, there is power and the anointing of authority.

What you are going through today in praying for your unsaved husband will build your faith, equip you, and give you authority to one day teach and encourage someone else. Much of the New Testament we have today is thanks to people like Paul who learned by experience how to handle extremely difficult trials and circumstances. What he learned, and the relationship he developed with the Lord, enabled him to teach and encourage many others through the letters he wrote that have been preserved for us today.

Difficulties, trials, and tribulations are like the bit of grit that forms the pearl in the oyster shell. It starts out as just an irritating bit of grit that has worked its way into an oyster shell and is rubbing up against the oyster. To overcome the irritation, the oyster secretes a substance that builds up, layer upon layer, over that bit of grit until it becomes smooth and more comfortable to live with—in fact it becomes a pearl.

In biblical times the pearl was considered far more valuable than gold or silver. Gold and silver were easily mined in quantity, but diving for pearls meant they were a rarer commodity. That's why Jesus spoke in a parable about the kingdom of heaven being like a pearl. "The kingdom of heaven is like a merchant looking for fine pearls. When he found one of great value, he went away and sold everything he had and bought it" (Matt. 13:45–46).

Our trials and difficulties are designed so that we produce "kingdom pearls." Jesus has already sold everything he had to buy the field—the rest is up to us.

SPECIAL NOTE

Joy Dawson has written a book called *Intercession: Thrilling and Fulfilling* and a booklet called "How to Pray for Someone Near You Who Is Away from God" (© YWAM, PO Box 55787, Seattle, Washington, USA), both of which contain her teaching on this subject. I contacted her and she has given me permission to quote from these sources in order to help you in your praying. As the story progresses I will insert her quotes as appropriate.

CHAPTER 30

"Remind Him of You, Lord"

Joy Dawson once wrote,

> Ask God to reveal himself to them in a personal way that they cannot refute and bring them to a realization that by becoming a Christian they have everything to gain and nothing to lose.

"Remind him of you, Lord," became a standard prayer. "Wherever he is, whatever he is doing." The trouble is that when you can't see what your man is doing or what he is looking at or what he is thinking about, you often don't know if this sort of prayer is being answered.

Bill would sometimes ask me questions about God and the church, but then the shutter would go down and I would have to wait for the next opportunity. Sometimes a long time would pass with no spark of interest from him at all. This would leave me feeling that it was hopeless, that he wasn't interested at all and would never become a Christian.

But as the despair rolled over me, I would cry out to the Lord for some encouragement. And out of the blue Bill would say something like "You'll never guess who came into the shop today. It was one of those black Gospel preachers. He was saying 'Hallelujah!' and 'Praise the Lord!' all over the place."

As he neared Damascus on his journey, suddenly a light from heaven flashed around him. He fell to the ground and heard a voice say to him, "Saul, Saul, why do you persecute me?"

"Who are you, Lord?" Saul asked.

"I am Jesus, whom you are persecuting," he replied. (Acts 9:3–5)

We all long for our unsaved husbands to have a Damascus road experience, where they will encounter the Lord and hear him speak to them, but that is a very rare occurrence. What is much more likely, and happens a lot more frequently, is that they will have lots of little Damascus road experiences—times when the Lord reminds them of himself in different ways and situations.

After Bill was saved I found out that the Lord had regularly spoken to him gently. There was a set of traffic lights at the top of a hill that Bill had to pass through on his way to work. Almost every day the lights would turn red just as he got to them. Opposite the lights, on the other side of the road, was a church, and outside the church was a billboard. This billboard (good name, huh!) was regularly updated to display a witty or pointed Christian message. Often Bill would be at the front of the line, and there was nothing he could do but stare at the message as he waited for the lights to change to green. It happened so frequently that eventually even he began to realize that the Lord was trying to get his attention!

"Lord, please save him!" was my usual way of praying, but now I was being challenged to think about that prayer. Did I just want Bill to be saved, go to church every Sunday and then to heaven when he died? No, I didn't. That sounded very boring and unproductive. In my heart I was sure that this battle for his salvation would result in far more than that. Also, I had read the parable of the sower, and I didn't want the seed of his salvation to spring up in shallow soil. So how do you pray for a "good harvest"? I thought of everything I would like to see happen—that he would be baptized in water, be filled with the Holy Spirit, be discipled, be obedient, and so on. Then I realized I could sum it all up very easily: "Lord, I pray that he will put you first in everything."

> "Ask and it will be given to you; seek and you will find; knock and the door will be opened to you." (Matt. 7:7)

Ask for what you want. Don't be vague—be specific and be bold. But ask for the sake of the Lord's kingdom and for his glory. Let us be wives who want a good harvest, a good return for our sowing. Part of the waiting time we go through in praying for our husbands is because the soil needs to be properly prepared. The ground has to be plowed in prayer; the seed has to go deep into the dark soil of their hearts. Then it needs the water of the Word and the warmth of our love and the light of the "Son" to have its good effect.

> For at the proper time we will reap a harvest if we do not give up. (Gal. 6:9)

I found the following quote from Joy Dawson's writing to be helpful:

> Our spiritual ambition for the extension of God's Kingdom will be manifest by the way in which we pray for the lost.
> We can be satisfied with praying just for their conversions, or we can pray that they will be converted and become deeply committed disciples of the Lord Jesus. We can pray that they will have a burning desire to know God and make

him known, and impact their generation in the power of the Holy Spirit. We can pray that from their steps of obedience to revealed truth, they will be among the overcomers as described in the book of Revelation, and be a part of the Bride of Christ.

CHAPTER 31

Hungry for the Word

I would pray faithfully every day that Bill would become hungry for the Word. Day after day, I would pray the same prayer. As far as I knew it was having zero effect. Bill remained totally disinterested in my Bible and, as we never went out without each other apart from his work, I was pretty sure he never went near it. How wrong can you be!

> We should therefore pray that God will bring his word to them or take them to his word and give them a desire to read it. He has numerous ways of answering that prayer. Just believe that he will. (Joy Dawson)

After Bill was saved we were talking to some friends about our experiences in those difficult days, when suddenly I heard Bill say, "In those months before I was saved I was so restless at night that I would get up and wander about the house. I would open Mo's Bible and I would read her notes. One day she had written all about hell, and I found myself reading about hellfire and worms eating you. Ugh, it was horrible!"

I nearly fell off my chair! I had faithfully prayed that Bill would be hungry for the Word, but I never saw any evidence that my prayer was being answered. But God must have waited for me to be in a deep sleep and then nudged Bill awake for a "night prowl." Bill was too proud to admit that he was curious about what I was reading and writing, so he never told me what he'd been doing. And I would get up the next day and pray yet again for God to make him hungry for the Word, totally oblivious that my prayer was already being answered!

> Now faith is being sure of what we hope for and certain of what we do not see. (Heb. 11:1)

Discouragement is so often linked to what we don't see. So many negative thoughts come to our minds like, "You're wasting your time! What do you think you are achieving with those empty words? God's not listening and he's certainly not answering your prayers!"

You may not be able to see any evidence at the moment, you may be discouraged, and you may be thinking your prayers aren't being answered, but then again, maybe they are!

CHAPTER 32

It's the Ministry

As I prayed for my husband, a recurring thought would hinder my prayers. It went something like this: *You only want him to be saved so that you can have an easier life; so that you won't have all these hassles and arguments; so you can go to church and be a nice Christian couple like everyone else.* This was all very true, and I would come away from my prayer time feeling guilty. Was I just being selfish?

"How do I handle this, Lord? These thoughts are robbing me of my confidence in prayer!" The answer the Lord gave me was to pray not just for Bill, but for the ministry that was contained within Bill. My husband could be a potential evangelist who would lead thousands to the Lord. He might one day be a great preacher or teacher who would inspire the people of God or be used in healing the sick. The thoughts of what ministry may be hidden away within him were endless, but God knew exactly what he had planned for Bill's life. So I began to pray for Bill to be saved, not for my convenience, but for the release of God's ministry contained within him.

Wow! What a difference it made. No longer was I plagued by those negative thoughts. I had removed the ground of accusation of selfish praying, and I was now praying on God's behalf, and my confidence, and subsequently my faith level, increased.

You may be familiar with the story in the Bible about Joseph.

"Here comes that dreamer!" they said to each other. "Come now, let's kill him and throw him into one of these cisterns and say that a ferocious animal devoured him. Then we'll see what comes of his dreams." (Gen. 37:19–20)

Jealousy and hatred in the hearts of Joseph's brothers provoked them to try to murder the dreamer in order to destroy the dream. It wasn't so much the dreamer that was the issue—it was the purposes of God that were contained within him!

But what they didn't realize was that those dreams, those purposes of God contained within Joseph, would mean their own salvation. The brothers were the descendants, the seed of Abraham, whom God had covenanted to bless and multiply. They were the ones out of whom would come the nation of Israel and eventually the promised Messiah.

And it's the purposes of God contained within our loved ones, not just their own salvation, that is at stake in our prayer battle. It's their ministry, how God will use them when they are saved, that is at the heart of it all. And all are unique in how they will fulfill the destiny or dream that is contained within them and how they will affect others around them. Joseph was used not only to save the lives of his family and the nation of Israel, but he was used to feed and save millions of others in the process.

If people are kept in spiritual darkness and death, then the ministry, the purposes of God contained within them, is also kept in darkness and death—it is rendered inoperative and ineffective! But, praise God, our loved ones can be saved from the pit; they can come out of prison and may even be promoted to a position of prominence. And whatever their ministry, as they fulfill the purposes of God for their lives, they will certainly affect and influence many others for good. Then we, and they, like Joseph, can say, "You intended to harm me, but God intended it for good to accomplish what is now being done, the saving of many lives" (Gen. 50:20).

CHAPTER 33

God's Perspective

One of the things I'd written down in my notes from the Joy Dawson meeting was, "Ask the Lord how he feels about being rejected by your loved one." So in my prayer times I would ask to understand—from God's perspective not just mine. Nothing happened for a while. I could think about how he might feel, but I knew that to pray effectively I needed to have the revelation in my heart. I also knew I wasn't to be half-hearted about wanting to know, so I persisted in praying this prayer often. Then one day the revelation came. I don't know why it was that day and not another, but the important thing was it came.

It broke my heart to see Bill's rejection of the Lord's offer of salvation from God's perspective, but to try and describe it to you would be irrelevant, for you need to understand for yourself. All I can say is it made a great deal of difference to the intensity of my prayers for Bill from then on. Now I could understand and identify with both God and man.

For we do not have a high priest who is unable to sympathize with our weaknesses, but we have one who has been tempted in every way, just as we are—yet was without sin. Let us then approach the throne of grace with confidence, so that we may receive mercy and find grace to help us in our time of need. (Heb. 4:15–16)

Jesus could have stayed in heaven and prayed for us, but he didn't. He came to earth as a man so that he would know exactly how we feel; so that he could understand the pressures and temptations we go through. This makes his intercession for us now very powerful!

And in the same way that Jesus became like us to understand what it was to be human, we too need to understand just what it's like for the Lord when his offer of salvation is rejected. We need to know how he feels.

To be an intercessor for a husband, or anyone else, we have to "stand in the gap." That means we have to stand in the middle and represent both parties, totally unbiased and able to understand both points of view—like a negotiator in a dispute.

The difference between prayer and intercession is that prayer is like standing in a corner of a room looking across and sympathizing with the people in the opposite corner and then talking to God about them, whereas intercession is actually standing in the same corner with them, knowing how it feels, identifying with them, and crying out to God on their behalf. Intercession is deeper; it's as if it's happening to you!

Remember those in prison as if you were their fellow prisoners, and those who are mistreated as if you yourselves were suffering. (Heb. 13:3)

If you were held in a prison or were being made to suffer, you wouldn't be passive—you would cry out with your whole being! So to intercede effectively we need to see God's perspective and identify with him as well—to stand in his corner too. Then when we know the pain in the Lord's heart at the rejection he feels, it will cause a great cry for mercy to go up to the throne of grace.

In Exodus 32:7–14 we read how God became really angry, because the children of Israel, the people he had chosen to be his own, the people he had delivered out of Egypt and out of slavery, had made an idol of gold in the shape of a calf. After all that God had done for them it was no wonder that he said to Moses, "Now leave me alone so that my anger may burn against them and that I may destroy them. Then I will make you into a great nation" (v. 10).

Moses could have said, "You are right, Lord. They don't deserve to live. Yes, make a great nation from my descendants instead." But he doesn't, and neither does he say, "Oh God, they didn't mean it. Please forgive them."

Instead, Moses takes the position of an intercessor. He stands "in the gap" between the people and God. He represents both parties and identifies with God and identifies with man.

First, Moses reminds God of his character and his glory: "Why should the Egyptians say, 'It was with evil intent that he brought them out, to kill them in the mountains and to wipe them off the face of the earth'?" (v. 12). Then he reminds God of his covenant promises to Abraham, Isaac, and Jacob (Israel), and all that he had sworn to do through their descendants—not just through Moses!

> "Remember your servants Abraham, Isaac and Israel, to whom you swore by your own self: 'I will make your descendants as numerous as the stars in the sky and I will give your descendants all this land I promised them, and it will be their inheritance for ever.'" (Exod. 32:13)

When we understand God's perspective we can, like Moses, remind God of his character and his glory, so that those around will see and marvel at what a great and merciful God he is. Despite man's rejection of such an amazing salvation, his character is such that "mercy triumphs over judgment!" (James 2:13).

Then we can also remind him of the covenant promises he gave to us—the promises that are for all of his New Covenant people, as written in his Word, as well as the promises that have been given to us specifically.

CHAPTER 34

Removing Hindrances

Earlier on in the book I spoke about the mistake I made in thinking that, because I was saved in a meeting, I needed to get Bill to a meeting so that he, too, could be saved. Later on I realized this was just one of the hindrances I had lodged in my subconscious, because another way I learned to pray was, "Lord, is there anything in me that is causing a blockage to Bill's salvation?"

You have to be prepared for the answer when you pray a prayer like that! Over a period of time the Lord began to reveal all sorts of blockages. I realized that many of my motives for Bill being saved were very self-centered. During that time the Lord also revealed to me my pride, my unbelief, my prejudices, and my wrong attitudes.

As the days went by I realized the Lord was challenging me to examine myself in regard to the aspects of relinquishment in Joy Dawson's teaching. Did I really mean it when I said to God, "Use anyone, anywhere, under any circumstances, to bring Bill to you"? Or, "Lord, if after his conversion you should call him to a foreign mission field, or he is martyred for you and I face the possibility of never seeing him again, then that's okay. He is in your hands for the present and the future"? Or even, "If by my death Bill could be brought to you, Lord, then I'm a candidate for death. Bill's salvation means more to me than life"?

I knew for me to pray without any hindrances, and for God to be free to answer in any way he wanted to, I had to renounce, to give up, all the ways I thought Bill would be, could be, or should be saved. I had to relinquish my timetable and my dictating to God as to the when, where, how, and by whom of his salvation. I also had to let the Lord examine my heart and reveal any wrong attitudes toward Bill for not responding to the Lord and against the Lord for not answering my prayers.

As I gave up my conscious and subconscious desires, prejudices, and attitudes, it purified my motives and enabled me to pray more according to what the Lord wanted—for his sake and not mine!

> When you ask, you do not receive, because you ask with wrong motives, that you may spend what you get on your pleasures. (James 4:3)

> Christ will be exalted in my body, whether by life or by death. For to me, to live is Christ and to die is gain. (Phil. 1:20–21)

I don't know if I would have prayed so often and so earnestly for Bill to be saved if he hadn't caused me so much difficulty, or if our lives and his attitude toward me hadn't been so radically turned upside down. But many of my legitimate earthly pleasures and comforts disappeared overnight, and pleasure, or lack of it, is a great motivator.

But our pleasure and comfort is not the basis for prayer for salvation. It not only hinders God's plans and purposes, but it leaves us vulnerable to condemnation. The accusation of selfishness robs us of confidence before the throne of grace, and we are open to feelings of guilt instead.

That's why we need to be open to hear from God about any hindrances in our lives, so that we can pray positively and with confidence, and so that our faith can grow as we see that what is left is a purer motive.

> He shall see of the travail of his soul, and shall be satisfied. (Isa. 53:11 KJV)

CHAPTER 35

Cutting the Strings

God now began to say that it was time to cut the strings that were manipulating Bill. As I thought and prayed about this I realized that, on the day we were married, Bill and I became one in God's sight. Jesus said, "For this reason a man will leave his father and mother and be united to his wife, and the two will become one flesh. So they are no longer two, but one" (Mark 10:7–8).

I was Bill's wife and therefore one with him in the flesh, but we were not yet one in the Spirit. So as part of him I felt called to resist the Enemy who was pulling the strings and manipulating some of Bill's behavior, in order to free his mind and his will to understand and respond to the truth.

> God opposes the proud but gives grace to the humble. Submit yourselves, then, to God. Resist the devil, and he will flee from you. (James 4:6–7)

The Lord had already been teaching me about submission, relinquishment, not holding unforgiveness, walking wisely, and so on, and I could see how important it was to have all that in place so that I had the authority to resist the Enemy. Jesus had provided me with his armor, so now it was up to me to make sure I continued living in all that he had shown me, to take up the sword of the Spirit, which is the Word of God, and use it to begin cutting those strings.

Every day I would take my stand against the Enemy with my "sword" in my hand—or rather in my mouth. Not just once or twice but again and again, cutting through those thick strings that were holding Bill. I would wield that sword and resist the Enemy at any time, wherever I was, whatever I was doing—in my prayer time, washing up, peeling the potatoes, or having a bath. I wasn't a mighty warrior or some spiritual giant. I was just a young housewife and a young Christian, but I was doing the next thing the Lord told me to do. He gave me the commission and I fulfilled it, not in isolation but in the context of all that he was teaching me, plus all the other ways I had learned to pray.

Sometimes my old selfish nature would trip me up and make me ineffective in the battle. But each time I would repent, say, "Sorry, Lord," and get back into the fight.

> Finally, be strong in the Lord and in his mighty power. Put on the full armor of God so that you can take your stand against the devil's schemes. For our struggle is not against flesh and blood, but against the rulers, against the authorities, against the powers of this dark world and against the spiritual forces of evil in the heavenly realms. (Eph. 6:10–12)

When we resist the Enemy, we must do so as the Lord directs. But first we need to make sure that we have the full armor of God firmly in place, as described in Ephesians 6.

We need to put on the belt of truth—especially the truth of his faithfulness and power—but also remember to ask the Holy Spirit to speak truth to us.

Then we need the breastplate of Jesus' righteousness to cover our heart. Our righteousness is no good; it cannot withstand the arrows of accusation. And we need the helmet of the hope of salvation to keep our mind protected and at peace.

We need to take up the shield of faith. The Hebrew word here is *thureos* and refers to a shield the size and shape of a door—so big that we can stand behind it. It was oiled to keep it supple, and that oil of anointing will quench the flaming arrows of the Evil One.

We need the sword of the Spirit—the Word of God—to defend our position and to resist the Enemy. And we need to have our feet prepared with the Gospel of peace, ready to move at his direction, treading wisely and with peaceful intent.

Our mouths must be filled with prayers and requests of all kinds, keeping in constant touch with the Commander of the army as we serve him in this way.

And then we must stand: stand our ground and stand firm because the Enemy's aim is to cause us to fall—fall for his temptations and tricks.

So we are to "be strong in the Lord and in his mighty power" (v. 11). We must put on the full armor that he provides, then stand and wrestle, throw down an enemy that is unseen but very real, being aware that we are in a wrestling match against spiritual forces, not man—flesh and blood. We must be bold, but totally under the Lord's command, and fight as he directs, in his strength.

It's very important that we don't fight in our own human strength, spurred on by our emotions. We must take our stand abiding in him, continuing in him, in covenant with him, established in him. Then we can wield the sword of the Word to set the captives free, to cut the strings and release their will, so they can then make free choices of attitude, behavior, and action.

The reason the Son of God appeared was to destroy the devil's work. (1 John 3:8)

I will build my church, and the gates of Hades will not overcome it. (Matt. 16:18)

There are many scriptures that the Lord can and will give you to cut those strings. Some may be well known, and some may be new to you and specific for your situation. Just ask him. Then pray those scriptures, putting in the name of the person you are praying for.

For instance, I used Psalm 3:7–8 to pray, "Arise, O Lord! Deliver Bill, O my God! Strike all his enemies on the jaw; break the teeth of the wicked. From the Lord comes deliverance. May your blessing be on Bill." And Romans 5:19 to pray, "For just as through the disobedience of the one man Bill was made a sinner, so also through the obedience of the one man Bill will be made righteous."

This will be a wrestling match, and there may be days when you feel the Enemy has you on the mat. Sometimes I would feel depressed for no particular reason, or discouraged and wonder what on earth I was doing. But this is all part of the struggle. Don't give up—ask the Lord for encouragement; ask the Holy Spirit to speak truth to you. Check that you haven't taken off your breastplate, and get behind that great big shield. Finally, use that sword again and again and again, because the best weapon for defense is attack.

We are not called to be perfect in order to fight in this battle. But we are called to be obedient to the Commander of the army. I was only a young Christian when I had to learn to fight, and I certainly wasn't perfect. The amount of rubbish that's been removed from my life since then is mind-boggling. I often wonder how God could have used me when he knew all the imperfection that was in me. But he did, simply because in his sight I was righteous through Jesus' death and no other reason. And the lessons I learned then about submission, relinquishment, walking wisely, wrestling, and so on, all have to be constantly practiced now, many years later, because the flesh and the Enemy are always contending for the ground that's been won.

CHAPTER 36

Trust and Obey

Now that I was going to church every Sunday morning, I had something else to worry about! What was Bill doing on Sunday mornings while I was at church? Because when he saw that he couldn't deter me from going, he began to take on an air of indifference, and sometimes secretiveness, as if to say, "You're not getting the upper hand on me. I have other things to do than wait indoors all morning for you to get back from church!"

Going to church for me was an act of obedience, not defiance. So I had to remind myself of the scripture, "Take captive every thought to make it obedient to Christ" (2 Cor. 10:5).

If I had given my thoughts free rein I would have worried myself silly and may have been tempted to obey them rather than obey the Lord. So all I could do was trust God with the consequences of my obedience and pray for divine intervention.

I did this by following Joy Dawson's excellent teaching. I prayed

1.   That the Lord would reveal to Bill the absolute reasonableness of surrendering his will to him, by giving him an understanding of his true character.

2. That God would put the fear of the Lord on Bill and that he would restrain him from evil, because as the Scripture says, "… through the fear of the LORD a man avoids evil" (Prov. 16:6).

3. That I would have peace of mind by putting into practice Psalm 37:5: "Commit your way to the LORD; trust in him and he will do this." The Hebrew word for *commit* literally means "to throw." We need to throw our loved ones onto the Lord. As Joy Dawson says, "The Lord has the ability to catch them, knows how to work on them for their best interests, knows the best methods and timing, will only do the right thing and just thing by everyone concerned, and longs to catch them anyway."

> Therefore, prepare your minds for action; be self-controlled; set your hope fully on the grace to be given you when Jesus Christ is revealed. (1 Peter 1:13)

Because we have no way of knowing what our loved ones are doing when they are out of our sight, all we can do is pray and trust them into God's hands. Our imaginations will only lead us into fear and anxiety. We need to prepare our minds, be self-controlled, and set our hope on the grace of God. Or as the King James Version translates 1 Peter 1:13: "gird up the loins of your mind."

To "gird up your loins" means to tuck your long garment into your belt in order to run without tripping. It's to make sure that, as you run the race he's called you to, all that is loose and liable to flap around in your mind is safely tucked into the belt of truth.

Not only do we need to pray for the fear of the Lord to be on our loved one, but we need to have the fear of the Lord too. This word *fear* means "reverence" or "deep respect." It's different from panic. The word *panic* comes from "Pan," the name of an ancient god who was believed to cause terror. What we want is the awesome respect that is evoked by a good father who causes his children to walk wisely for fear of the consequences.

The Bible tells us that the fear of the Lord has some wonderful benefits:

> The LORD has compassion on those who fear him. (Ps. 103:13)

> Surely his salvation is near those who fear him. (Ps. 85:9)

> Through the fear of the LORD a man avoids evil. (Prov. 16:6)

> The fear of the LORD is the beginning of wisdom. (Ps. 111:10; Prov. 1:7; 9:10)

> To fear the LORD is to hate evil. (Prov. 8:13)

That's the sort of fear we need, and so do our loved ones: a fear that will enable them to know his compassion, his salvation, and his wisdom so that both we and they may avoid evil because we hate it.

Finally, I found a wonderful verse in Isaiah about the fear of the Lord: "The fear of the LORD is the key to this treasure" (Isa. 33:6).

CHAPTER 37

Is This It?

With my new intensity of prayer, coupled with the steps of obedience, relinquishment, and cutting the strings, a day finally
came when Bill was more open to talk than I'd ever known. He began
to ask questions and to listen to the answers.

"Maybe I'll try this Christianity stuff," he said.

"Really?" I eagerly replied. "If you want to become a Christian, you
need to pray a prayer saying that you are sorry for all the wrong things
you have done and then ask Jesus to come into your heart and life. Do
you want to do that?"

"Um, okay, but I'm not praying out loud," he said.

So I told him what to say and waited while he prayed silently.

"Have you prayed?" I said, a minute or two later.

"Yes, I've prayed," he said.

"Oh good. You can come to church with me tomorrow, then!"

"No, I don't think I'll do that. Maybe another time."

Oh. That didn't sound too promising.

"I don't think your heart's fully in this, Bill. You can't sit on the
fence on this issue, and if you don't decide properly the Enemy will just
grab your leg and pull you back down on his side!"

And that's precisely what happened. After a few days his attitude began to worsen again, and within a week he was acting aggressively, as if nothing had happened.

As you can imagine, I was very disappointed. But having seen that new openness, even for such a short time, I realized I wasn't wasting my time. So I continued in prayer with an even stronger determination to keep on until I knew Bill really was the Lord's.

> Perseverance must finish its work so that you may be mature and complete, not lacking anything. (James 1:4)

At the time I would have given anything for Bill's prayer for salvation to be real. But afterward, when I realized he had only paid lip service to becoming a Christian instead of really repenting and asking the Lord to come into his heart and life, I was glad that his lack of commitment was so obvious. It would have been awful to have a husband with a half-hearted commitment to the Lord. I could see that a lukewarm response would have made life just as difficult but in a different way.

As I have told this story and thought about that particular episode, I have come to the conclusion that things don't just suddenly change. There is a slow process of change going on in those we are praying for. Every now and again we are given an encouraging glimpse. It's the same with our faith; it increases imperceptibly, and we don't realize it till we look back.

It's like the tide coming in. The waves are going in and then out. They don't just go in and in—there is a rhythm to their progression, back and forth, back and forth, but the end result is progress. Similarly with our faith, there are movements forward and then movements backward, but imperceptibly the tide is steadily coming in. Then, just as we think that this time the wave will go all the way to the top of the beach, we find that it falls short. Not only that, but it seems to recede even further back than before! But don't be fooled, because the stronger the wave pulls back, the stronger it will return to crash higher up the beach. Don't give up—be encouraged, for the big one is just about to happen!

Rejoice with Those Who Rejoice

As I continued earnestly to persist in prayer for Bill every day, throughout the day, I heard that a young couple in our town had come to our church and been saved. Then not long after that another young couple and a young man were all saved within a very short time of each other.

My immediate reaction was anger and jealousy. Why them? And why so suddenly out of the blue? No one in our church had been praying for them as far as I was aware; and I, and the church, had been praying for my husband for ages. Here was God pouring out salvation on these strangers without all the hard work of persistent, consistent prayer—or so it seemed.

As the anger and jealousy arrived in my heart, so did the Holy Spirit with his gentle, insistent nudging. "Don't go down that path. It only leads to bitterness and destruction." I knew that he was right, and so I struggled with my angry reasoning, desperately crying out to him to help me win this battle.

Then the thought came clearly to me, *If God is pouring out his Spirit of salvation "over there," he could just as easily pour it out "over here" too!* So I began to thank him and praise him and encourage him to do just that. As I did so, faith began to well up in my heart. Now instead of going down that negative, destructive route, I was going up and up in the joy that these people had been saved. God was working in our town—hallelujah!—and Bill was on his hit list, so it shouldn't be long now!

> Rejoice with those who rejoice. (Rom. 12:15)

It's so easy to become angry and jealous when you have been faithfully praying all to no avail, or so it seems. There is so much injustice in this world, both real and that which we experience because of our own agendas—those false expectations of action and timing. And just as we react to man's injustices, so can we react to what seems like injustice from the God who says he loves us and is committed to us.

But this is part of trust—to accept that he alone knows the agenda and the timing that is right for our particular situation. And negative reaction and attitude is like a blockage in the pipe—it stops the flow! We must give him our disappointments and then pray and react positively.

It was just after this time that the Lord drew my attention to Psalm 37.

> Commit your way to the LORD; trust in him and he will do this: He will make your righteousness shine like the dawn, the justice of your cause like the noonday sun. (vv. 5–6)

> For the LORD loves the just and will not forsake his faithful ones. (v. 28)

CHAPTER 39

An Unforgettable Weekend

It was just an ordinary Saturday night. The girls were in bed, and Bill and I had settled down to watch a film on the television. The opening scene in the film was a man climbing up a telegraph pole, and as he reached the top he accidentally touched a wire. He was immediately electrocuted and fell to the ground, dead! One minute he was alive and the next minute he was dead! I turned to Bill in the chair beside me and said, "That could be you, you know. You could be dead tomorrow, and you'd go straight to hell!"

Bang! It was as if I'd shot him with a gun.

"No!" he said. "That can't be right! You mean I'd go to hell with murderers and rapists? That can't be right. There must be a third alternative for guys like me!"

I assured him that there wasn't, and if he didn't want to go to hell then he'd better get his life in order. He'd better become a Christian.

I have set before you life and death, blessings and curses. Now choose life, so that you and your children may live and that you may love the LORD your God, listen to his voice, and hold fast to him. (Deut. 30:19–20)

The timing of that film and its dramatic opening was the Lord's doing. I had no idea that I would say what I did, or that it would have such an impact. We can plot and plan what we think needs to be said and when, but when the Lord gives the opening, it's perfect.

I didn't have any idea that it was "the night before," either, but God did!

I realize now that my statement, as unpretentious and as simple as it was, was a "Jericho shout," because those thick and impenetrable walls that were keeping Bill from knowing the truth of the Gospel cracked—and were about to come tumbling down!

THIS IS THE DAY

The next morning as the girls and I got ready to go to church and Sunday school, Bill said, "I won't be in when you get back. I'm going out and I don't know what time I'll be home!" He sounded so self-assured and secretive.

"Oh dear, Lord," I whispered, "help me not to think about what he might be up to. You know all about it, so I give him back into your hands again." And off I went to church.

Before the service began they announced there was to be a baptismal service again that evening. Someone else had asked to be baptized after last Sunday evening's baptismal service, so the sensible thing to do was to leave the pool where it was and baptize them this Sunday evening. Instead of having Communion as usual in the evening, therefore, they would have it at the end of that morning's service. This way it wouldn't inconvenience anyone who had to leave the church on time, and any others who weren't in a hurry could stay on and take it.

Well, I reasoned to myself, *if Bill's going to be late back from wherever he's gone I might as well stay and take Communion.* So I did.

It was the day before my mom's birthday, and we were due at my parents' home for lunch. To my surprise, Bill was waiting when Jan dropped us off at home, so the children and I jumped into our car with him and drove off to my parents' house. There was a moment during that afternoon when Bill and I were on our own and he said, "I have something to tell you, but not now."

Oh dear! I thought. *What's coming? Oh please, Lord, help me. Give me the grace to know how to handle it if he's found another woman!* Once more I had to look away from the possible consequences of being obedient.

We returned home fairly late that evening, put the children to bed, sorted things out for the next day, and then sat down in the lounge.

"So, what was it you wanted to tell me?" I asked.

"Um, er, why don't you make us a drink and I'll tell you in bed?"

So we sat in bed with our drinks and I waited …

"Well, you know I said I was going out this morning and would probably get back late?"

"Yes," I replied.

"Well, actually, I didn't go out at all. I was only saying that to make you think I wasn't bothered about what you were doing; that I had other interests of my own. It was all just a bluff, a ruse to get you worried. In fact, I sat at home all morning reading the Sunday newspaper. When it was about the time you were due home, I got in the car and drove around the town, and then I walked indoors expecting to find you there worrying and fretting over where I was. But you weren't home!"

"I stayed on to take Communion thinking you wouldn't be home till later," I said.

"Well, anyway, thinking I'd mistimed it, I got back in the car and drove around the town again, came home, walked through the door, but you still weren't there! This time I was really bothered, because unless I got back after you, my whole plan to get you upset and anxious would be wasted. So I got back in the car and drove around the town for a third time. Thinking you must surely be home by now, I came home and confidently strolled in to find, yet again, an empty house! I got into the car for the fourth time and just as I was about to switch on the engine again, I said to myself, 'What are you doing? What are you trying to prove? You know you can't shake her! You know she's right, and you know you want what she's got!' So with that I got out of the car and waited for you to return."

"This is amazing!" I said. "Do you mean that you want to give your life to the Lord? To become a Christian?"

"Yes, I guess I do."

Into my mind came the time, a few months previously, when he thought he might try "this Christianity stuff" and ended up sitting on the fence after "praying in his mind." So I said, "If you mean it, you'll get out of bed, get down on your knees, and pray after me."

To my utter amazement he said, "Okay" and got out of bed.

He prayed after me, asking for forgiveness and asking the Lord Jesus to come into his heart and life. He then sat on the bed and said, "Is that it? Am I a Christian now? Has the Lord come into my life?"

He hadn't had a tangible experience of the presence of the Lord coming upon him as I had when I was born again, but he had spoken the name "Lord"—and meant "Lord"—for the first time in his life.

> If you confess with your mouth, "Jesus is Lord," and believe in your heart that God raised him from the dead, you will be saved. For it is with your heart that you believe and are justified, and it is with your mouth that you confess and are saved. (Rom. 10:9–10)

Can you believe it? After all my dreaming about how Bill would eventually be saved, when it happened it was nothing like I imagined at all. He never went near a church or a meeting, he never heard a sermon, didn't get drawn in by the praise and worship like I did. He didn't have an experience of the Lord's presence coming upon him—no "Damascus road" revelation, no deathbed commitment, no passing evangelist coming into the shop.

It was just the final wave hitting the top of the beach. It was the accumulation of all that had gone on before—the prayers that had been prayed, cutting the strings, the relinquishment, the steps of obedience, and the fear of the Lord. They'd all had their impact and had gathered momentum to bring him to this final point of realizing that he, too, wanted what I had—a relationship with the most loving and powerful Person in the whole universe.

CHAPTER 40

The Next Day

It was Monday morning. Bill got up early and went to work, and I was left to get the girls ready for school. As I walked to school I shared with Jan the amazing events of the day before. She was so excited, but I felt very uneasy. Here I was telling her that Bill had become a Christian, but inside me there were incredible doubts. Had he really meant what he had said last night kneeling on the bedroom floor? What if he hadn't? The doubts went on and on as the news went around the church like wildfire. People were phoning each other with the good news, that after all their prayers, Bill Tizzard had given his life to the Lord.

Later that day I went with Jan to visit the young couple who had recently been saved, and I remember feeling absolutely miserable because I felt like an impostor. Inside I kept thinking, *He didn't really mean what he said. He'll come home tonight and he won't be any different. You are going to feel such a fool when you have to tell everyone it was a false alarm.* What I thought would be the happiest day in my life was ruined by these awful doubts.

So when Bill eventually came home I was holding my breath. But as I looked at his face, it was so different. He was smiling and his eyes were clear and bright—no shutters now—and he gave me a big hug. It was true! He had meant what he had said and prayed! What a relief! All that doubt was a product of my own fear and totally unfounded.

"I must go and ring David and Jan Dixon before I do anything else," Bill said. "I can't forget how rude I was to them when they came here last year about that psychiatrist thing. I must apologize."

As David later told us, "I knew it was a genuine conversion as soon as I picked up the phone and heard Bill's apology. It was obvious evidence of a repentant heart."

"I tell you that in the same way there will be more rejoicing in heaven over one sinner who repents than over ninety-nine righteous persons who do not need to repent." (Luke 15:7)

There was certainly rejoicing in heaven and on earth that day, and I wish I had been able to join in earlier. After all that time of praying and waiting, it was hard for me to believe that it had actually happened. We always imagine what will happen and how we will feel, and I think it's often our romantic notions that spoil us for reality. But it's reality that we have to live with and so I want to give you an accurate picture. It's like giving birth. Having looked forward to the day and imagined how wonderful it will be when the baby arrives, when the day comes there is more involved than the joy of the arrival!

NEW BEGINNINGS

I don't remember much about the next few days except for the mixture of joy and anxiety. For just like when that first newborn baby arrives, it's a whole new situation. I knew where I was with an unsaved husband. I had gotten used to a certain way of living. Now it was a whole new ball game, and neither of us knew exactly how to handle it. I wanted him to be the spiritual head of the house, but at that moment he was a spiritual baby. What was I to do? I remember thinking that maybe I should take it slowly as a Christian, hold back and give him a chance to catch up. I had learned an awful lot in a short time because of him, and so there was a gap between us in spiritual growth. No sooner had those thoughts come into my head than the wisdom of the Holy Spirit spoke clearly to me through the verse—and the song— "Seek ye first the kingdom of God, and his righteousness; and all these things shall be added unto you" (Matt. 6:33 KJV).

I knew then that I should continue growing and developing as a Christian, being obedient to and keeping my eyes on the Lord and trusting him to take care of the growth of his newborn son.

On Friday evening it was the church prayer meeting, so Jan babysat for us so that we could both go together. We walked into the hall to find all the chairs were taken except for some in the front row, so we had no choice but to sit there. Bill was absolutely amazed that everyone knew him. They greeted him like a long lost brother—which I suppose he was! At a certain point in the meeting they announced that we were going to pray for the unsaved husbands of the women in the church, which they had been doing regularly each week for a long time. Bill turned to me and said in a very loud whisper, "Is this the point where I was prayed for?" and the whole meeting collapsed in laughter. They had also been regularly praying for more musicians, too, which Bill was, so he had actually been receiving a double dose of prayer most weeks!

Everyone seemed full of joy that night. Here was Bill, sitting among them after all that praying. At the end of the meeting they were almost queuing up to shake his hand and say hello. He was a bit overwhelmed but nevertheless delighted to be received so warmly. I, on the other hand, was having a struggle. I had suffered so much abuse and rejection from him throughout the whole time I had been a Christian, and now all that seemed to be forgotten, and here was Bill being accepted as if nothing negative had happened. I knew my attitude was totally wrong, but there it was, like a big black cloud blocking out the sun, robbing me of the joy that my prayers had been answered at last.

> The heart is deceitful above all things, and desperately wicked: who can know it? (Jer. 17:9 KJV)

I told you I would give you the accurate picture, and I hope you aren't too shocked. But the reality was that, as I looked into my heart, I realized there was a part of me somewhere deep down that wanted justice and maybe even revenge. I wanted people to realize and sympathize with what I had gone through!

It is so much a parallel of giving birth to a natural baby. When you are expecting, everyone is concerned with how you are doing, but when the baby is born they are totally taken up with the new infant. They fuss over him, saying how cute he is, who he looks like, how much he weighs. In the joy of his arrival, most people are oblivious to all the agony you've just gone through to bring him into the world.

It sounds bad, doesn't it? But it's often so true. We are selfish creatures, and if unchecked, our hearts harbor all sorts of nasty thoughts and attitudes. Well, you'll be glad to know that I didn't let the night pass before I repented. While Bill was talking to someone else, I slipped into another room to pray with a motherly lady named Pat James. I confessed my rotten thoughts and my seeming ingratitude, and I received God's forgiveness and cleansing. Then and only then was I able truly to rejoice over Bill's salvation.

That evening, through the people of God and their unconditional acceptance and welcoming of Bill, I saw in action the following scriptures:

> Who is a God like you, who pardons sin and forgives the transgression of the remnant of his inheritance? You do not stay angry forever but delight to show mercy. You will again

have compassion on us; you will tread our sins underfoot and hurl all our iniquities into the depths of the sea. (Mic. 7:18–19)

As far as the east is from the west, so far has he removed our transgressions from us. (Ps. 103:12)

And for myself, the next few verses of this psalm were very appropriate: "As a father has compassion on his children, so the LORD has compassion on those who fear him; for he knows how we are formed, he remembers that we are dust" (Ps. 103:13–14).

CHAPTER 41

God's Timing Is Perfect

One of Bill's objections to going to church had been that, in his opinion, it was full of little old ladies with buns and glasses. Well, was he in for a shock! That Sunday morning, as we arrived at church, his eyes nearly bugged out of his head. For young people were there, with long hair and wearing jeans. Most of the members of our church were far from old and were smartly but casually dressed; but this Sunday was the beginning of a month of outreach in connection with a group of young people from Youth With A Mission. They had come to work alongside our church in evangelism.

They were from different nationalities, and some of them were musicians, and led the worship that morning with their guitars. Bill was taken up with the joy and enthusiasm they radiated. Instead of being bored, as he had always thought he would be, he thoroughly enjoyed it all.

When we were at the Friday night prayer meeting, Jill and Malcolm Jackson had invited our family to their house for Sunday lunch. We were both delighted when we found they had also invited several of these young people from Youth With A Mission—YWAMers. Included in the invitation were the group leaders, an American couple named Pete and Dawn Burkhart. Bill and Pete took to each other immediately and spent a lot of the afternoon talking together.

For the next four weeks the YWAMers opened a coffee bar in the church fellowship hall every evening to attract the town's young people. Bill went there every night that he could, with his guitar. He would talk to people about the Lord, play his guitar, and learn some Christian music.

As I told you in the previous chapter, the church was praying for musicians, especially guitar players. The person who usually played the organ for the hymns at church was a very dear lady named Amy Lansley. She was an older, single woman who had a bun and wore glasses! But she was no fuddy-duddy; in fact her favorite trick was to sing, "I want a man …, I want a man …, I want a mansion in the sky!" The pastor, David Dixon, had tried to update the music in the church, and being the only musician himself, apart from Amy on the organ, he would play the choruses on the piano, then go up and preach the sermon, returning to the piano to play again if necessary. But now it looked as if Bill might be the answer to their prayers, not just as a newly saved husband, but as a guitar player as well!

> And we know that in all things God works for the good of those who love him, who have been called according to his purpose. (Rom. 8:28)

As the title of this chapter says, God's timing is perfect. Within three weeks of Bill being saved, Pete Burkhart prayed with him to be filled with the Holy Spirit. Then after the YWAMers left, Bill went through a discipleship course with some of the other new Christians, and soon he was there welcoming people on the door as they arrived at church and leading the worship!

CHAPTER 42

Yes! God Does Want to Save Your Man

O ne of the hardest things to cope with when praying for an unsaved husband is the nagging question, "Does God want to save him? Is it God's will?" That question can go round and round in our minds, undermining our confidence in prayer.

When Jesus died on the cross, he died for the whole of mankind. He died for your husband too, to bring him into restored relationship with the Father and to know forgiveness of his sins. The problem is, and always has been, not with God's will but with man's! The offer of salvation is held out, but will he take it? That is the real question!

I have pondered a lot over the years about why more women than men respond to the offer of God's salvation through Jesus Christ. I believe it's because most women are more sensitive and intuitive and they are natural responders, whereas men are more mind-oriented; they need concrete facts and they prefer to initiate.

But let me encourage you—the Lord sees a husband and wife as one. When the Holy Spirit sends forth the light and revelation of the Gospel to a wife, he is not just seeking to save her, but he is seeking to save both partners. Men tend to avoid the light and revelation of the Gospel. They often won't put themselves under the spotlight by attending church or Christian meetings. They don't give much opportunity for Jesus to knock on the door of their lives. But by saving the wife, I believe Jesus goes around to the back door, so to speak, in order to shine that light more fully. He gives the husband the opportunity to see the truth in his wife and to respond to Jesus' knocking.

The desire of the Lord is that the light will grow brighter and brighter, so that a man cannot deny the truth anymore and will respond to the offer of salvation.

> The lamp of the LORD searches the spirit of a man; it searches out his inmost being. (Prov. 20:27)

> "No one lights a lamp and hides it in a jar or puts it under a bed. Instead, he puts it on a stand, so that those who come in can see the light. For there is nothing hidden that will not be disclosed, and nothing concealed that will not be known or brought out into the open." (Luke 8:16–17)

We are usually unaware of the brightness of the light coming from our spirits, but our husbands aren't. Some men adopt the stance of tightening their blindfold and declaring, "What light? I can't see any light!" While others, like my husband, yell at the tops of their voices, "Turn that light off!"

But be in no doubt—the light from your spirit is exposing the darkness, and the closer you get to the Lord, the brighter it will shine!

> For God, who said, "Let light shine out of darkness," made his light shine in our hearts to give us the light of the knowledge of the glory of God in the face of Christ.
>
> But we have this treasure in jars of clay to show that this all-surpassing power is from God and not from us. (2 Cor. 4:6–7)

CHAPTER 43

Ripples on the Pond

I cannot finish this book without telling you of some of the ripples that have occurred since Bill's salvation. To begin with, that very first week, I had a phone call from another wife in the church whose husband wasn't saved. Kathy Palmer rang to say how pleased she was for me that Bill had been saved. She had been praying for her husband Mike for two years, and he was the total opposite of Bill. He never minded Kathy going to church or meetings. In fact, because she couldn't drive, he would take her where she wanted to go and then return home again. I think he considered her churchgoing a hobby; he had his hobbies and she had hers.

After I had put the phone down, I thought, *It was so nice of her to phone, but she must be feeling terrible, wishing it was Mike who had been saved. I know I would if it was the other way around.* So I picked up the phone and rang her back, and she immediately burst into tears. I arranged for her to come round, and I shared with her the ways I had been praying that I had learned from the "how to pray for unsaved loved ones" meeting. She wrote down everything and went home with new ammunition.

After eight weeks of Kathy putting these things into practice, continually resisting the Enemy and being obedient to what God told her to do, Mike became a Christian. He, too, was a musician who played the guitar, and Bill and Mike became like brothers in the Lord. They did everything together, led worship together, and went through discipleship together. They came into house group leadership at the same time, and both ended up in church leadership in the years to come.

I have to tell you that at the time of my salvation I was just twenty-five years old and Bill was thirty. He was saved eighteen months later, and he has been a Christian now for twenty-eight years. In that time he has led and taught worship, as well as other subjects, in several places in the world. He has been the full-time leader in a church, and together we have led Crossroads Discipleship Training Schools for those over thirty years of age in Youth With A Mission. He is still playing the guitar, leading worship in our local church, and taking outside opportunities that still keep coming in.

We have shared this testimony of how Bill was saved many, many times, especially when we were in YWAM—at the beginning of each new school in testimony time. But it is only now that God has said to write it down. I hope it is of use to you in giving you encouragement in ways to live and pray. My prayer is that the ripples will go on and on and on ...

Readers' Guide

FOR PERSONAL REFLECTION
OR GROUP DISCUSSION

Introduction

Quite likely you will read this book because of your desire to pray for your unsaved husband, friend, or relative. The following chapter-related questions will aid you in your journey of prayer and hope, courage and uncertainty, discovery of God and searching self-discovery.

You'll explore:

- Key issues mentioned in the chapters,
- Your expectations of what you'd like God to do,
- Dependency on God and attributes of his character,
- Your need of other believers' prayerful support,
- The dangers of resentment and bitterness,
- The joys of seeing God at work.

You'll also be challenged to go deeper in your walk with God, who wants to teach us himself so we become "bonded" to him.

As you answer the questions, you may cry … laugh … pray … praise … and rethink truths you thought you knew. That's part of the process of praying earnestly for an unsaved loved one and growing to know God in a much deeper way.

If you are tempted to give easy answers to some difficult questions, pause and reflect. As Mo discovered, special insights and experiences often result from wrestling—with questions, with ourselves, with God. As challenging as the following questions may be, they reinforce the hope, joy, and peace God promises. Jesus identifies with your weaknesses and offers help. He loves your unsaved spouse, friend, or family member. He wants to renew and guide you.

There's no "right way" to use these questions. You might spend lots of time thinking about one question, then move through others more quickly. Or find yourself branching off into prayer, Bible reading, or discussion with a Christian friend after a question connects with you in a special way.

May God bless you during this journey, drawing you closer to him as you intercede for those he loves. Let the light of Christ shine through you, and always remember that he is faithful and "able to do immeasurably more than all we ask or imagine, according to his power that is at work with us" (Eph. 3:20).

CHAPTER 1

1. Why do some people react so negatively when they learn their spouses have become Christians and want to attend church?

2. What kinds of reactions have people you know had when their spouses became Christians?

3. Why are you reading this book? What would you like God to do in your life and in the life of your husband?

4. How can we each gain the assurance that we are God's child and are part of his family?

CHAPTER 2

1. Why do you think Mo's relatives and family tried so hard to get her to change her mind about being a Christian? When they encouraged her to go back to being "normal," what did being normal look like to them?

2. What and/or who do you think gave Mo the courage to stand up for her newfound faith?

3. Do you think Mo answered correctly when she agreed not to go to church or any more meetings, and not to do anything more with the friend who invited her to go there? Why or why not?

4. How should we respond when influential, well-meaning people closest to us try to talk us out of following Jesus, believing they have our best interests at heart?

CHAPTER 3

1. What did Mo discover about prayer?

2. What role did Jan choose to have in Mo's life? And how did Jan's loving commitment affect Mo?

3. How does what Mo learned about depending on God relate to us today, whether or not we are in similar situations?

4. What causes some Christians to lose the joy they first had in talking with Jesus?

5. As it related to her time with God, what did Mo learn about the importance of distinguishing between what is urgent and what is important?

CHAPTER 4

1. What did Mo learn as she read the Bible?

2. Why did Jesus choose to die on the cross? And what opportunity do each of us have as a result?

3. Mo wrote, "I knew then that his [God's] love was unconditional." What is this unconditional love, and why did it mean so much to her?

4. What is your concept of God? Have you, like Mo, discovered that he—the loving heavenly Father—offers unconditional love and forgiveness from your sins? What does John 3:16 reveal about him?

CHAPTER 5

1. Why do you think the church devoted so much energy to praying for Mo and her family?

2. What does Exodus 17:8–13 reveal about how much each of us needs the support of other Christians? Where can we find people who will stand with us and encourage us, the way Aaron and Hur helped Moses?

3. "We need to be dependent, resting, abiding, and putting all our weight on him [Jesus]," Mo wrote. In practical terms, what does being dependent, resting, abiding, and putting all our weight on Jesus really mean? What are some examples of this?

4. At the end of this chapter, Mo cautioned us not to become resentful or bitter. Why are resentment and bitterness so dangerous?

CHAPTER 6

1. How can we demonstrate to our families that we are Christians? How do we show them more of God and less of ourselves? (If you are reading this book with a group, and you feel comfortable doing so, share what you are learning about this.)

2. What does it mean to be "filled" with the Holy Spirit?

3. Why do we need to be continually filled with the Holy Spirit? What happens if we try to share Jesus, live the Christian life, and pray effectively without His presence working in and through us every day?

4. Do you find it easier to share Jesus with complete strangers or with those you know and love? Why?

5. What are the hardest things you face as you try to live out your faith in Christ in front of your family?

CHAPTER 7

1. Why do we find it easy sometimes to set up our own "master plans" for how God will work in someone's life?

2. What did Mo learn as a result of Bill's refusal to go to the meeting? In what ways can our strong desires for something lead us away from God's purposes and blind us to the truth?

3. How can we deal with the fact that God does things according to his will, not just the way we think he should do it? What does Romans 8:28 reveal?

4. How important is it for us to seek the Lord's forgiveness when we make foolish mistakes concerning our husbands? Why?

CHAPTER 8

1. Why do you think Mo's questions helped to break down walls of tension between her and Bill?

2. How does retaliation affect a marriage relationship? How can a spouse learn not to retaliate, like Mo did?

3. Do you agree that "walking wisely usually means talking wisely"? Why or why not? What does the second part of Matthew 12:34 teach?

4. When we speak negative words, what do we reveal about what's in our hearts? How does dwelling on the negative affect us—including our relationship with God? What is God's solution as recorded in Philippians 4:8? What are some examples of this?

5. Which tips did Mo share about how to work on improving the attitudes in our hearts and facing negative words and thoughts? If you are studying this book in a group, and you feel comfortable doing so, share how you have dealt with the challenge of negative attitudes, thoughts, and words.

CHAPTER 9

1. Where does our faith in what God can do come from?

2. How capable is God of answering our prayers, no matter how simple or complicated they may be? (Read Isa. 46:9–11.)

3. What does God use to build up our faith?

4. Mo wrote, "The increase of our faith is of greater value to our God than quick answers to prayer." Do you agree or disagree? Why? What does 1 Peter 1:6–7 reveal about the relationship of our suffering to our faith?

CHAPTER 10

1. Why was it important for Mo not to push Bill to allow her to be baptized—and then to keep praying?

2. What is the importance of baptism?

3. How does Proverbs 3:5–6 relate to what Mo was experiencing? To what you are experiencing?

4. Why do we use manipulation to try to "make something happen"? What does manipulation reveal about our view of God?

5. How does 1 Peter 3:1 relate to the "pray-and-wait" approach Mo began using?

CHAPTER 11

1. Read John 13:34–35. Why is it so important for Christians to love one another? Contrast what Jesus said here with the other ways some Christians try to set themselves apart from other people.

2. How do you think Jan's practical help impacted Bill? Why did he find her actions so difficult to ignore?

3. Mo wrote, "Words on their own don't mean very much. People want to see your words in action." What practical things can we do to demonstrate God's love to non-Christians and Christians?

4. Why should we pray for God-given opportunities to demonstrate his love instead of just coming up with ideas and plans on our own?

CHAPTER 12

1. How does reading the Bible regularly enhance our prayer lives?

2. How do you think Mo felt when God gave her a specific, encouraging Bible verse—2 Corinthians 5:7? How does this verse relate to our desire to see our husbands become Christians?

3. What does God want us to develop as we pray for our husbands and may not be seeing much happening? As we face times of darkness and barrenness?

4. Why do we need to develop deep "faith roots"?

5. How do you respond when you experience difficult times and find yourself losing hope?

6. What does Isaiah 50:10 reveal about how we should respond during times of darkness in our lives? What does this kind of trust look like? What are some examples of what it means to "rely" on God? (If you are studying this book with a group, and feel comfortable doing so, share an example from your own life.)

CHAPTER 13

1. Why may a believer's faith in God provoke jealousy in his or her unbelieving spouse? Where can the believing spouse turn to for counsel on what to do when such jealousy arises?

2. Bill used verbal abuse to try to "shock" Mo out of being a Christian. Do you think he was looking for an intellectual response to his attacks, or something else? Why?

3. Why did defending herself make Mo's situation with Bill worse?

4. What does 2 Corinthians 2:14–16 reveal about the impact of Christians in daily life?

5. Imagine you are a non-Christian who knows little, or nothing, about the Bible and ways of God. How would you feel and respond if your beloved spouse started talking to you about church and God, using words you didn't understand, and behaving differently? (Be honest!) What insights does this provide concerning trials we face in our marriages because of our faith?

6. What does it mean to be thankful for trials we experience because of our faith? In what way(s) is being thankful during these situations contrary to the flow of our culture? Contrary to how we may feel like responding?

CHAPTER 14

1. Do you think Mo was surprised by what happened after she told God she'd put up with anything if it meant Bill would find Christ? Why or why not?

2. Read 1 Corinthians 10:13. Then think about a time when you "couldn't take it anymore," and God helped you. Did he change you? Change circumstances? How can what you've learned in the past about God's faithfulness apply to your current or future testing times?

3. How do we know for sure that Jesus identifies with our struggles and will help us during our weaknesses?

4. Jesus counted the cost of coming to earth and being crucified for our sins, and he refused to come off the cross when religious leaders mockingly challenged him to do so. Sometimes, as we try to obey God during difficult times, we are tempted to "come down off the cross of God's will" for our lives. How can we hold onto the hope we have in our mighty risen Savior?

CHAPTER 15

1. When you hear the word *fasting*, what comes to mind? Why?

2. What, according to Mo, is the relationship between prayer and fasting? What cautions did she share regarding fasting?

3. How might you learn more about fasting and its significance?

CHAPTER 16

1. Why is it important for us to read the Bible regularly? (See Ps. 119:130.)

2. In what way(s) did the Holy Spirit reveal truth to Mo?

3. Based on Ephesians 1:17, what may we ask God to give us?

4. Read Ephesians 4:22–23. What does it mean to be renewed in the spirit (attitude) of our minds?

5. What does reading God's Word prepare us to receive?

6. How can we differentiate between the wisdom (James 3:17) and guidance the Holy Spirit provides and the thoughts that are not from him?

CHAPTER 17

1. Have you ever just had "chats" with the Lord at various times during the day, telling him how you feel about things and asking him what to do? Why or why not?

2. What are some obstacles we must overcome in order to pay attention to the actions God wants us to take and to the way he wants us to pray?

3. After hearing what she believed was truth from God, Mo sought confirmation through wise Christian friends. Why?

4. What does it mean to "wait on God"?

5. When Mo strained to hear from God, what happened to her? And what did she learn as a result?

CHAPTER 18

1. Why is our relationship with God so important to him?

2. What cautions did Mo offer concerning our search for answers to our problems?

3. "Seek the Lord for the blueprint for your own particular situation," Mo wrote. What happens when we emphasize methods rather than allowing God to guide us step by step?

4. What insights do Joshua 5:13–15 and Isaiah 48:17 give us concerning God and our obedience to him?

CHAPTER 19

1. What's the difference between praising God for all circumstances and praising him in all circumstances?

2. Despite Bill's criticism and negativity, what did Mo praise God for . . . and how did her praise affect her life? Her level of faith?

3. How does Philippians 4:4–7 relate to your life? What wonderful promise is found in this passage?

4. According to Philippians 4:6, how are we to present our requests to God?

5. What does 2 Chronicles 20:1–30 reveal about the effectiveness and power of praise?

6. Read Psalm 48:1. To what extent should our emotions—how we feel— influence our praise of God? Why?

CHAPTER 20

1. How did Mo's recognition of who was behind Bill's unkind actions affect her ability to love Bill?

2. Why is it so important for us to deal with our wounds quickly so they don't "fester into bitterness"?

3. What three steps did Mo learn to do when Bill's attacks hurt her deeply? How might these make a difference in your life?

4. Why is there such power and healing in forgiving those who "fire wounding arrows" at us?

5. How do the contrasts mentioned in Isaiah 61:3 relate to us today?

CHAPTER 21

1. What can we learn about forgiveness through what God did for us when we became Christians? (See Eph. 4:32; Ps. 103:12; Isa. 43:25.)

2. Why is the confession of our sins so important as we seek to forgive other people (including our spouses) for the wrongs they have done to us?

3. What is the price we pay for unforgiveness?

4. How does understanding that forgiveness is an act of the will, not a feeling, affect our choice to forgive other people?

5. Which point(s) stood out as you read the seven steps to forgiveness? Why? What will you do this coming week to start implementing these steps, if you are not already doing so?

6. What can we do to make forgiveness "a way of life"?

CHAPTER 22

1. Why do we need to recognize that we will make mistakes as we learn to discern God's opportunities?

2. What are some ways by which we can know when our spouses, or other loved ones, are asking sincere questions about the things of God and his

kingdom? (If you are studying this book with others, and you feel comfortable doing so, share something you've learned about this.)

3. What happens when we try to force spiritual issues on our husbands rather than discerning God's opportunities? When we respond to comments designed to provoke us?

4. How does Luke 11:34–36 relate to discerning God-given opportunities to share his truth?

CHAPTER 23

1. When the moods of others around us are turbulent, what can we do to "stay level" and remain fairly peaceful? What does John 15:5 reveal? How might praising God help us to keep focused and trusting in him?

2. What is involved in taking control of our reactions?

3. Why is it important for us to remember that Satan wants to frighten us and make us anxious, unfruitful, and unproductive? What kinds of things might we pray for so we can be alert to his wiles?

CHAPTER 24

1. Read John 14:16–17 and John 16:13. How do they apply when a spouse or other loved one accuses you, and the bit of truth in the accusation takes away your sense of peace?

2. What keeps us from asking the Holy Spirit to illuminate the darkness in our lives, reveal any deception being used against us, and help us sort out the confusion that condemnation brings?

3. What's the difference between the Holy Spirit's conviction after we make mistakes and people's condemnation of us? Why is it important, as Mo discovered, to understand the difference? How can condemnation keep us from accepting God's forgiveness?

4. Do you think each of us deserves to be forgiven by God? Why or why not? What is the only basis for his forgiveness?

CHAPTER 25

1. How did God use Mo's act of love to break down barriers between her and her husband when she didn't think she loved him anymore? What does Galatians 5:6 reveal about what really matters?

2. What's the relationship between love and faith as they relate to your marriage?

3. When your human resources dry up and your emotions get weary, how do you respond to your spouse? What did Mo learn about being honest with herself and with God in this situation?

4. Respond to this statement: "God alone is the source of our strength and the source of all wisdom. Only he can give us the specific instructions we need to carry on. Only he is on both sides at once, loving the husband and wife deeply and equally."

CHAPTER 26

1. When you read the word *submission*, what did you think? What did you feel?

2. What keeps us from being completely submissive to our husbands? To God? What does it mean to "submit," as the word is used in Ephesians 5:22?

3. How can we know when submission to a non-Christian husband clashes with submission to the Lord?

CHAPTER 27

1. How do you think Bill felt when Mo stated that she was going to do what the Lord told her to do?

2. As you face a difficult situation when you must face the cost of obeying God, how do you respond?

3. Mo wrote, "To be obedient [to God] will sometimes involve relinquishment." What did she mean? When did Jesus relinquish his will and his rights?

4. Which aspect(s) of your life do you have a hard time relinquishing to God?

5. Why can the Enemy no longer use anything we relinquish to God to create fear in our lives?

CHAPTER 28

1. How do you think Mo felt when she realized she was to go to church despite whatever Bill might say or do? On what did she focus her mind before leaving for church?

2. What comfort can we receive from Joshua 1:9?

3. How can we focus on God rather than on our fears? What are some areas in which we can trust God in spite of our fears?

4. How does God use our weaknesses to draw us closer to him?

5. How might our lives be different if we realize that when God tells us to do or say something he already has a plan worked out to take care of the consequences?

CHAPTER 29

1. How is our openness and brokenness before God and his people related to seeing his power at work in our lives?

2. Mo wrote, "What you are going through today in praying for your unsaved husband will build your faith, equip you, and give you authority to one day teach and encourage someone else." In what way(s) might God be preparing you to use what you are learning to teach and encourage someone else?

3. What kinds of "kingdom pearls" can our trials and difficulties produce in our lives?

CHAPTER 30

1. When we each pray, "Remind my husband of you, Lord," what are we asking God to do in our husbands' lives?

2. Why is it important for us to be available to answer whenever our husbands ask sincere questions about God and the church?

3. Why do you think God usually uses "lots of little Damascus road experiences" to remind our husbands of himself in different ways and situations? What kinds of situations and people might God be using in your husband's life?

4. What hope can we find in Jesus' promise in Matthew 7:7? What holds us back from being specific and bold when we pray for our husbands' salvation? What role does prayer play in cultivating the "spiritual soil" in our husbands' hearts?

5. Do you pray only for your husband's conversion, or that he will also become a deeply committed disciple of Jesus Christ? What might God be encouraging you to pray for?

CHAPTER 31

1. Have you, as Mo did, prayed that God will bring his Word to your husband or give him a desire to read it? Why or why not?

2. What gives the Bible such power?

3. Read Hebrews 11:1. When you become discouraged by what you don't see happening, what kinds of thoughts come to mind? Why is it sometimes hard during such times to focus on God's promises? On God's never-changing faithfulness and love?

CHAPTER 32

1. What types of thoughts rob you of your confidence in prayer?

2. How will our lives be different if we realize that God knows what he has planned for our husbands and that everything doesn't rest on our shoulders?

3. Why did Mo begin praying differently for Bill's salvation? Do you think her earlier prayers might have been selfish? Why or why not?

4. What's really at stake in our prayer battle, much more than our husbands' salvation?

CHAPTER 33

1. Mo persisted in asking God how he felt about being rejected by Bill. What do we communicate to God when we pray persistently for his will to be accomplished in specific areas?

2. What does Hebrews 4:15 reveal about God's perspectives on our struggles and hopes?

3. What is the difference between prayer and intercession? How did Moses demonstrate intercession in Exodus 32:7–14? Why do you think he first reminded God of his character and glory?

4. What do you think God feels when we remind him of the promises he has given us?

CHAPTER 34

1. Have you prayed and asked God to show you anything in yourself that is causing a blockage to your husband's salvation? What do you think of this idea?

2. Read James 4:3. What are some of the wrong reasons why Mo prayed for Bill's salvation? Which do you identify with?

3. "I had to renounce," wrote Mo, "to give up, all the ways I thought Bill would be, could be, or should be saved. I had to relinquish my timetable and my dictating to God as to the when, where, how, and by whom of his salvation." What did you think about when you read this?

4. Why are many Christian wives afraid to let God examine their hearts and reveal any wrong attitudes toward their husbands for not responding to God and toward God for not seeming to answer their prayers? How do such wrong attitudes affect our ability to pray positively and confidently?

5. How might praying that our husbands will become Christians for our pleasure and comfort hinder God's plans and purposes?

CHAPTER 35

1. Read James 4:6–7 slowly, focusing on each phrase. What might God want to tell you through these verses?

2. How can our prayers and love actually make a difference in helping our husbands' minds and wills understand and respond to God's truth?

3. Read Ephesians 6:10–17.

4. Where do we get the authority to use the "sword of the Spirit" to take our stand against the Enemy's attacks?

5. Which elements comprise the "full armor" of God? Why are each of these vital?

6. What do 1 John 3:8 and Matthew 16:18 tell us about the power of God?

7. Mo mentioned using passages of Scripture when she prayed. Have you ever done this? If so, what happened? If not, why not?

8. What suggestions did Mo offer us for the times when we feel depressed and discouraged? Why do we have to keep practicing what we've learned rather than growing complacent about spiritual battles taking place?

CHAPTER 36

1. What is involved in "taking every thought captive" to make it obedient to Christ? (See 2 Cor. 10:5.)

2. What happens within us when we trust God with the consequences of our obedience and pray for divine intervention?

3. Reread the three things to pray for on pages 145–146. How might you and your spouse's lives be different if you begin praying for these?

4. When we are tempted to worry about our husbands when they are out of our sight, what can we do, according to 1 Peter 1:13?

5. Read the following verses and consider the benefits for those who fear (have deep respect or reverence for) God:
   Psalm 103:13
   Psalm 85:9
   Proverbs 16:6
   Psalm 111:10
   Proverbs 1:7
   Proverbs 8:13
   Isaiah 33:6

CHAPTER 37

1. Read James 1:4. Why must we continue to pray for our unsaved husbands?

2. Why might no response from our husbands concerning spiritual things be better than half-hearted commitments?

3. Do you agree that usually things (and people for whom we pray) don't suddenly change? Why or why not? What practical things can we do when facing the usually slow process of spiritual change?

4. In the past, how did you respond when your situation seemed to worsen? What hope have you gleaned from this chapter?

CHAPTER 38

1. Why did Mo become angry and jealous after hearing about other people's conversions? Of what did the Holy Spirit remind her?

2. What role did praise have in helping Mo receive joy during this time?

3. If our husbands don't come to faith in God, does that mean that God—who says he loves us and is committed to us—is being unjust? Why or why not? (See Ps. 37:5–6, 28.)

4. Why do we sometimes find it hard to accept that God alone knows the agendas and the timing that are right for our respective situations?

CHAPTER 39

1. Why do you think Mo said what she said to Bill when the movie started? How did she know that the timing was right?

2. What gave Mo the strength to remain obedient to God, even if that might mean Bill would find another woman?

3. What did the events of this chapter reveal about God's perfect timing?

4. What does Romans 10:9–10 reveal about what's involved in becoming a Christian?

5. Having read all about Mo and Bill's experiences, what surprised you about Bill's decision to become a Christian?

CHAPTER 40

1. What doubts did Mo have to face?

2. In what way(s) did Bill evidence his newfound faith?

3. How does heaven respond when someone becomes a Christian? (See Luke 15:7.)

4. Why did Mo experience feelings of joy and anxiety? How did Matthew 6:33 help her?

5. As Mo reflected on all the abuse and rejection she had suffered, how did she feel? What does Jeremiah 17:9 reveal about why she felt that way? Why was it important for her to pray about those feelings?

CHAPTER 41

1. What surprised Bill when he first attended church?

2. As you read Romans 8:28, which events from Bill and Mo's marriage stand out?

3. How important do you think it was for Bill to become involved in the church soon after becoming a Christian? Why?

CHAPTER 42

1. Do you agree with Mo's reasoning about why more women than men respond to the offer of God's salvation through Jesus Christ? Why or why not? What could the church do to connect better with non-Christian men?

2. If your husband is not a Christian, how are you feeling right now? Why? What encouragement can you find in Proverbs 20:27 and Luke 8:16?

3. Read 2 Corinthians 4:6–7 slowly. Which phrases connect with you? Why?

CHAPTER 43

1. How will you apply what you learned in this book, whether or not your husband is a Christian?

2. If your husband is not yet a Christian, what will you do to draw closer to God? To continue to shine the light of Christ toward your husband? To seek wise counsel during times of discouragement?

3. If your husband has become a Christian, what will you do to draw closer to God? To encourage and help your husband grow in his faith? To reach out to wives who need to hear your story—what you've learned about yourself and God during the hard times as well as the good times?

The Word at Work Around the World

A vital part of Cook Communications Ministries is our international outreach, Cook Communications Ministries International (CCMI). Your purchase of this book, and of other books and Christian-growth products from Cook, enables CCMI to provide Bibles and Christian literature to people in more than 150 languages in 65 countries.

Cook Communications Ministries is a not-for-profit, self-supporting organization. Revenues from sales of our books, Bible curricula, and other church and home products not only fund our U.S. ministry, but also fund our CCMI ministry around the world. One hundred percent of donations to CCMI go to our international literature programs.

CCMI reaches out internationally in three ways:

· Our premier International Christian Publishing Institute (ICPI) trains leaders from nationally led publishing houses around the world.

· We provide literature for pastors, evangelists, and Christian workers in their national language.

· We reach people at risk—refugees, AIDS victims, street children, and famine victims—with God's Word.

Word Power, God's Power

Faith Kidz, RiverOak, Honor, Life Journey, Victor, NexGen — every time you purchase a book produced by Cook Communications Ministries, you not only meet a vital personal need in your life or in the life of someone you love, but you're also a part of ministering to José in Colombia, Humberto in Chile, Gousa in India, or Lidiane in Brazil. You help make it possible for a pastor in China, a child in Peru, or a mother in West Africa to enjoy a life-changing book. And because you helped, children and adults around the world are learning God's Word and walking in his ways.

Thank you for your partnership in helping to disciple the world. May God bless you with the power of his Word in your life.

For more information about our international ministries, visit www.ccmi.org.

Additional copies of *HOW TO PRAY WHEN HE DOESN"T BELIEVE*
and other Life Journey titles
are available from your local Christian bookseller.

If you have enjoyed this book,
or if it has had an impact on your life,
we would like to hear from you.

Please contact us at:

LIFE JOURNEY BOOKS
Cook Communications Ministries, Dept. 201
4050 Lee Vance View
Colorado Springs, CO 80918
Or visit our Web site: www.cookministries.com

Readers in Europe should write to:

Kingsway Communications Ltd
26-28 Lottbridge Drove
Eastbourne, BN23 6NT, UK
Or email: books@kingsway.co.uk.

LIFE JOURNEY®
Bringing Home the Message for Life